Sexual Violence and Humiliation

This book presents humiliation as a key harm of sexual violence against women, showing that humiliation manifests within the relation of self to itself, and that Foucault's critique of subjectivity provides resources for feminist conceptualization and countering of sexual violence and humiliation.

Within feminist philosophy and theory, rape and sexual assault are often described as humiliating to victims, yet relatively few in-depth feminist philosophical accounts and analyses exist of humiliation as a harm of sexual violence against women. This book provides such an account and analysis of both humiliation generally and sexual humiliation resulting from sexual violence more specifically. The book's elucidation of possibilities for countering sexual violence and humiliation, moreover, breaks with standard feminist approaches by critiquing rather than appealing to subjectivity. Through analyzing specific instances of anti-sexual violence protest, it shows that cultivation of alternative modes of self-relation furthers rather than undermines feminist efforts to combat sexual violence. Throughout, the book draws upon concrete, recent, and contemporary instance of sexual violence against women and feminist anti-sexual violence protest to illustrate and support its arguments.

This will become a key text for feminist scholars and Foucault scholars in the humanities and social sciences, and for graduate and advanced undergraduate students. It will also be of interest to feminist anti-sexual violence activists.

Dianna Taylor is Professor of Philosophy at John Carroll University in Cleveland, Ohio, U.S.A. She is co-editor of *Feminism and the Final Foucault* (University of Illinois Press, 2004) and *Feminist Politics: Identity, Difference, Agency* (Rowman and Littlefield, 2007), and editor of *Michel Foucault: Key Concepts* (Acumen, 2010).

Interdisciplinary Research in Gender

https://www.routledge.com/Interdisciplinary-Research-in-Gender/
book-series/IRG

Sexual Violence and Humiliation
A Foucauldian-Feminist Perspective

Dianna Taylor

Routledge
Taylor & Francis Group

LONDON AND NEW YORK

First published 2020
by Routledge
2 Park Square, Milton Park, Abingdon, Oxon OX14 4RN

and by Routledge
52 Vanderbilt Avenue, New York, NY 10017

Routledge is an imprint of the Taylor & Francis Group, an informa business

British Library Cataloguing-in-Publication Data
A catalogue record for this book is available from the British Library

Library of Congress Cataloging-in-Publication Data
Names: Taylor, Dianna, author.
Title: Sexual violence and humiliation : a Foucauldian-feminist perspective / Dianna Taylor.
Description: Abingdon, Oxon ; New York, NY :
Routledge, 2020. | Includes bibliographical references and index. |
Identifiers: LCCN 2019028259 (print) |
LCCN 2019028260 (ebook) | ISBN 9781138581432 (hardback) |
ISBN 9780429505423 (ebook)
Subjects: LCSH: Sexual abuse victims—Psychology. | Humiliation. |
Sex crimes. | Feminist theory. | Foucault, Michel, 1926–1984.
Classification: LCC HV6556 .T39 2020 (print) |
LCC HV6556 (ebook) | DDC 362.88301/9—dc23
LC record available at https://lccn.loc.gov/2019028259
LC ebook record available at https://lccn.loc.gov/2019028260

ISBN: 978-1-138-58143-2 (hbk)
ISBN: 978-0-429-50542-3 (ebk)

Typeset in Sabon
by codeMantra

MIX
Paper from
responsible sources
FSC   FSC™ C013985
www.fsc.org

Printed in the United Kingdom
by Henry Ling Limited

For Erinn Gilson, Debra Jackson, Qrescent Mason, and Merritt Rehn-DeBraal, with gratitude for their gestures of solidarity.

Contents

Acknowledgments

A number of friends and colleagues read and offered comments on the content of this book during the writing process, as well as provided encouragement and support more generally. Being able to meet together and discuss my work with Deniz Durmuş, Nathalie Nya, and Brenda Wirkus, my colleagues in the philosophy department at John Carroll University, and Malia McAndrew, my colleague in JCU's history department, generated valuable insights that enabled me to clarify my ideas and arguments. Conversations I had both individually and together with my former colleague, Namrata Mitra, and Clara Fischer about philosophy and life contributed to shaping the perspectives reflected herein; similar conversations with my colleague, Deniz, have been equally inspirational. Both Namrata and Clara also read and provided comments on drafts.

As I note in the book's conclusion, the National Endowment for the Humanities Institute in which I participated during the summer of 2017, Diverse Philosophical Perspectives on Sexual Violence, proved invaluable in moving this book forward. All aspects of that event – its organization and structure, the required readings, and especially the dedication and intellectual generosity of the scholars in residence and other participants – came together in a way that, for me, created an ideal space within which to think deeply as well as practically about the problem of sexual violence. Participating in the Institute also confirmed for me that what I wanted to write about that problem needed to be written. This confirmation came through learning from and conversing with scholars in residence Debra Bergoffen, Louise du Toit, and Nicola Gavey, upon all of whose work I draw. Especially valuable, meaningful, and memorable was the intellectual and personal camaraderie I enjoyed with the small group of feminist philosophers with whom I was fortunate to be assigned to work in a focused way during those two weeks, and to whom I have dedicated this book: Erinn Gilson, Debra Jackson, Qrescent Mason, and Merritt Rehn-DeBraal. I also greatly appreciate Erinn, Debra, and Merritt reading and commenting on drafts of various parts of the book.

For organizing and hosting the formative intellectual experience that was Diverse Philosophical Perspectives on Sexual Violence, I am deeply grateful to Ann Cahill, upon whose work I also draw in my analyses. Ann deserves my thanks as well for reading, commenting on, and supporting me in the approach I ultimately ended up taking in the book's Introduction, an approach which subsequently shaped the Conclusion in important ways.

Finally, I wish to thank Benjamin Fambrough for his support and patience while I persevered in completing this project.

Introduction

How much does it cost for victims/survivors to tell the truth?[1]

In the fall 2017, I attended a public forum of Ohio Democratic gubernatorial candidates that was held in the city where I reside. Audience members were invited to submit questions, and I did so. I was pleasantly surprised when my question, "Other than increasing incarceration rates, what steps will your administration take to reduce sexual violence against women and girls?", was actually raised. Less surprising (albeit disappointing) was the fact that while some responses the question generated were interesting (Dennis Kucinich quoting Gerda Lerner), none were particularly innovative or inspiring. After the forum was over, I thanked one of the moderators for including my question in the discussion. She indicated that sexual violence was an important issue. "It doesn't only affect women and girls, though," she elaborated. "Yes, I know," I replied. "But sexual violence against women and girls is an important issue for me, which is why I raised that particular question."

"In my discussions about the problem of rape in a variety of contexts, from the professional to the personal," Ann Cahill writes,

> my analysis of rape as a formational aspect of the daily lives of women has frequently been met with an insistence that men, too, are raped, and that therefore an emphasis on women as the sole victims of rape provides an inadequate portrayal of the problem at large.
>
> (2001, 124)

My analysis in this book, like Cahill's, focuses on sexual violence against women committed by men, a particular manifestation of what Susan Brison refers to more broadly as "gender-based violence against women by men" (2013, 259).[2] Brison invokes this terminology in order to express the reality that "no sexual violence is an isolated incident" (2017). Her conceptualization of sexual violence frames rape and sexual assault as systemic and vastly disproportionately committed by men against women simply because they are women. By situating sexual violence within the context of gendered power relations, Brison further points to its function, as I emphasize in the analysis contained in subsequent chapters, of enforcing women's subhumanity.

My exchange with the forum moderator was not the first time I have had an exchange similar to those Cahill describes. When I cover the topic of sexual violence in my courses, students inevitably raise the issue of male rape. Following Cahill's lead, I bring to their attention the fact that most victims of sexual violence are women, and I ask them to think about their "eagerness to claim for men an equal status of rape victim" (2001, 124). I also ask them to think about which men are targets of sexual violence and the specific contexts in which male rape most frequently occurs. Such prompting sometimes promotes critical reflection. The resentment with which it is also sometimes met is nothing, however, compared to the overt hostility a male philosopher directed at me during a conference session in which we were both presenters. He insisted that men experience sexual violence at the same rates as women and aggressively dismissed my analysis as discriminatory. "Patriarchy," Cahill writes, "has a stake . . . in representing rape as sexually neutral" (124).

This patriarchal masking of the gendered and systemic nature of sexual violence helps to explain the portrayal of #MeToo in the popular media as a calling out by particular women of the behavior of particular men, or perhaps of broader male behavior within particular industries (Walters 2018a). The speed, intensity, and scope of the response to actress Alyssa Milano's initial tweet, moreover, made #MeToo appear to have emerged "suddenly, out of nowhere," rather than as the most recent expression of women's long-held anger and frustration in the face of entrenched gender oppression (Hay 2017).[3] Anyone paying attention, Suzanna Danuta Walters argues in a *Washington Post* op-ed, would have been unsurprised by #MeToo and the anger it reflects; if anything is surprising, Walters contends, it is that broad-based expressions of women's rage don't occur more frequently. "My edge," she writes, 'has been crossed for a long time, before President Trump, before Harvey Weinstein, before "mansplaining" and "incels"' (2018a). Consistent with her framing of women's anger as a justified response to systemic gender oppression, Walters titled her opinion piece, "Why Can't We Hate Men?". While "admittedly framed in a provocative manner," the substance of her essay was, she asserts, "hardly debatable" (Ibid). After its publication, however, Walters received "hundreds" of death and rape threats; "some messages were so detailed and emphatic, the police had to look into them" (Ibid). A Title IX complaint was filed against her; calls were made for her to be fired. Walters's experience provides a more extreme illustration than my encounter with a hostile male philosopher of how women's drawing attention to and critiquing of gender-based violence against women by men is itself met with male aggression, including threats of (sexual) violence. "Sometimes," Walters reflects, "you really don't want to be right" (2018b).

I am completing work on this book in the shadow of the hearings that ultimately resulted in Brett Kavanaugh's confirmation to the U.S. Supreme Court. Those hearings and events surrounding them bring into sharp relief the systemic sexism and misogyny that generate conditions for the possibility of and are in turn reasserted by sexual violence against women. Anyone paying attention would not have been (as so many were) questioning why Dr. Christine Blasey Ford didn't report or readily speak out about her experience of sexual assault; rather, they would be wondering why any women, especially victims/survivors, ever speak out at all. After Ford, who was about to be identified in the media, publicly came forward and accused Kavanaugh, her email was hacked, her personal information was posted online, and she received death threats that forced her and her family to leave their home. All aspects of her life were scrutinized, and she was subjected to public ridicule and derision that escalated when she was questioned before the Senate Judiciary Committee, questioning that itself ranged from paternalistic to overtly hostile. Doubt was cast on Ford's ability to accurately and truthfully recount her own experience. Something happened, it was generally agreed, but all these years later no one could know for certain what. The only thing that could be known with certainty, apparently, was that whatever happened to Ford, it didn't happen at the hands of Kavanaugh. Even though most victims/survivors don't face either the extraordinarily public or the extraordinary degree of backlash Ford did, many don't tell anyone about their experiences of sexual violence. Many victims/survivors (rightly, as Ford's experience illustrates) don't think they will be believed. Many want to erase the memories of being attacked. In the face of criticism that her recollection of the assault was not crystal clear, Ford told a friend, "I've been trying to forget this all my life, and now I'm supposed to remember every little detail" (Williamson et al. 2018).

Humiliation, the focus of this book, is a key factor contributing to victims'/survivors' reticence and silence. My analysis shows that humiliation generally and sexual humiliation resulting from sexual violence more specifically foster a deeply negative relation of self to self, as well as a view of oneself as deserving to experience oneself in such a way.[4] It threatens, in other words, to establish a permanent self-relation of abjection. The potential to constitute, understand, and relate to oneself in such a way results from the internalization of normative negative external perspectives and treatment, internalization that occurs because our relationship to ourselves is formed in and through broader norms and practices, as well as our relationships with other people. Put differently, the experience of humiliation results from internalization of external humiliating conditions, perspectives, and treatment. Ford's internalization of sexist/misogynist views of women and the humiliation inflicted by sexual assault – that she was not only subjected to but actually experienced sexual humiliation, in other words – is apparent in her response to Senator Patrick Leahy's question concerning what she recalled most vividly about being sexually assaulted. "Indelible in the hippocampus," Ford replied, "is the laughter, the uproarious laughter, between the two [Kavanaugh and his friend Mark Judge]. And their having fun at my expense" (U.S. Senate hearings 2018).

Given that, following Foucault, I view the relation of self to self as the locus of both the proliferation and countering of normalizing and therefore potentially oppressive relations of power, my analysis in the following chapters details how humiliation functions in the service of normalization and oppression by undermining critical and creative capacities that facilitate both self-transformation and social transformation more broadly. As I show through my analyses, gendered relations of power both generate and legitimize women's general and sexual humiliation. Systemic sexism and misogyny reflect (and reassert) a normative view of women as inferior beings that leads to (and fosters legitimation of) their abusive treatment, of which sexual violence is a key manifestation. A view of women as inferior underpins the overt expressions of hostility, doubt, dismissal, and condescension that confronted Ford after she publicly accused Kavanaugh of sexual assault. Insofar as they cast Ford, as Judith Butler puts it, as a less than "fully livable life," those expressions reinforce her ostensible inferiority and, therefore, the conditions for the possibility of both her sexual violation and normative ambivalence in the face of it (2010).

In this book, I show that sexual humiliation resulting from sexual violence not only inhibits women's speaking about experiences of rape and sexual assault but also, and more fundamentally, exacerbates challenges with which victims/survivors grapple in making sense of those experiences for themselves. These challenges stem from the fact that during an attack, victims are temporarily reduced to attackers' perspective and abusive treatment – they are reduced, in other words, to their own humiliation and therefore rendered temporarily unintelligible to themselves. After the attack, victims/survivors find themselves in the position of having to rely upon concepts that are relevant to a context where one is not so reduced and thus once again intelligible to oneself (even if one's relationship to oneself has been compromised) to try to make sense of and communicate that reduction and unintelligibility. This situation is analogous to that with which, Hannah Arendt argues, concentration camp survivors were confronted upon their liberation. The unprecedented nature of the camps, according to Arendt, undermined fundamental concepts upon which human beings rely to make sense of their existence in the world, including the concepts of life and death. Prohibiting "[g]rief and remembrance," as was done in the camps, effectively erases death, with the result that lives which are no more cannot be acknowledged as having been meaningful existences (Arendt 1973, 452). In the face of this radical undermining of prevailing modes of meaning-making, survivors struggled with a severe disconnect relative to their own experiences. People were effectively invoking concepts to try to make sense of what had taken place within a context that undermined the efficacy of those very concepts; they were trying to grasp experiences defined by the meaninglessness of life and death from within a context where those concepts were meaningful. The horror of the camps, Arendt writes,

> can never be fully embraced by the imagination for the very reason that it stands outside of life and death. It can never be fully reported for the very reason that the survivor returns to the world of the living, which makes it impossible for him to believe fully in his own past experiences. It is as though he had a story to tell of another planet, for the status

of the inmates in the world of the living, where nobody is supposed to know if they are alive or dead, is such that it is as though they had never been born.

(1973, 444)

Arendt describes how the struggle for meaning by those who "resolutely returned to the world of the living" was further complicated by the "suspicion" with which their accounts were met (439). While she attributes this response to deep unease generated by being confronted with the limits of human understanding as well as the nature of the accounts that produced that confrontation, other factors may contribute to it as well. The discounting of survivor testimony may in part be an effect of what Graham Dawson refers to as "state-organized forgetting" – a collective desire to return to "a less painful normality" that disavows the oppressive source of painful experiences; it may also be an expression of resentment at being confronted by embodiments of one's own complicity with a system of genocidal oppression, or simply of overt Anti-Semitism (Dawson 2008, 72).

Within the context of gendered relations of power, state-organized disavowal deflects and denies the need for critique of systemic sexism and misogyny that produce and legitimize gender-based violence against women by men. Such disavowal therefore needs to be seen as underpinning practices like victim-blaming and minimization that reflect and reassert a view women as subhuman, treat them as if they are nonhuman, and thereby reinforce the ambivalence with which accounts of sexual violence are met. As Butler (2010) argues, lives deemed less than fully livable are not seen as fully injurable, with the result that harms against them are not fully recognized. Like Arendt, Butler considers grief to be a key expression of the recognition of livability. "Only under conditions in which [a] loss would matter," Butler writes, "does the value of life appear . . . grievability is a presupposition for the life that matters" (14). Responses that refuse to critically engage conditions for the possibility of grievous harm and therefore the nature of that harm itself, as I emphasize throughout this book, are normalizing. By allowing for the reproduction of those conditions and that harm, such responses implicitly validate both. They thereby exacerbate victims'/survivors' struggle to make sense of the experience of sexual violation and humiliation and further inhibit both recognition of sexual violation and humiliation as injuries, and efforts to communicate that struggle and that violation. In short, normalizing responses redouble victims'/survivors' humiliation.

Counter-normalization is a central theme and aim of this book. In what follows, I identify possibilities for, elucidate, and endeavor to promote counter-humiliating, oppositionally transformational interventions into and hence disruption of gendered power relations. Given its function as a key locus of both proliferation of and opposition to normalizing power, the relation of self to self must itself be interrogated, and counter-normalizing/counter-humiliating modes of self-relation cultivated, as part of such critical analysis and the broader counter-normalizing intervention onto which it opens. Although Foucault questioned whether, given prevailing conditions within the modern West, such cultivation was possible, he nonetheless critiques the relation of self to self in his late Collège de France courses. "How is it," Foucault asks in 1980, "that, in our type of society, power cannot be exercised without truth having to manifest itself, and manifest itself in the form of subjectivity?" (2015, 75). He provides, specifically, a genealogy that both reveals modern Western subjectivity to be a contingent and normalizing mode of self-relation and explores conditions for the possibility of alternatives, as well as possible forms those alternatives might take. In the West, Foucault shows, establishing a relationship to oneself has always been bound up with establishing a relationship to the truth. Since Descartes, constituting oneself in terms of truth has functioned to validate, valorize, and therefore reproduce the self-relation (of subjectivity) in its current iteration. Through an extended analysis of the ancient practice of *parrhēsia* or "truth-telling," however, Foucault elucidates a subversive manner of constituting a mode of self-relation in terms of truth. This parrhesiastic mode of self-relation gives expression to truths that prevailing modes of meaning-making and power relations have suppressed or otherwise rendered unintelligible. Constituting oneself in terms of unpopular truths entails the taking on of risk, including the risking of one's own intelligibility; it is therefore characterized by courage.

As I acknowledge in Chapter 1, critiques of subjectivity by privileged white male philosophers have, for good reason, never sat well with feminists. Subjectivity is conceived and experienced not as a particular mode of self-relation, but as a necessary ground of both intelligibility and meaningful action. Feminists have tended to equate subjectivity with recognition as a fully livable, rather than subhuman, life; it is tied not only to intelligibility but also to resistance and emancipation. The frequent framing of the harm of sexual violence in terms of objectification, moreover, instills the status of subject with enhanced significance. Contra these perspectives, in what follows I show that humiliation generally and sexual humiliation more specifically manifest within the self-relation by means of and therefore redouble defining normalizing mechanisms through which subjectivity establishes itself as a necessary condition of intelligibility and meaningful action. In light of this normalizing interconnection between subjectivity and (sexual) humiliation, I make a case for "loosening" feminist "attachments" to subjectivity as a mode of self-relation; such loosening entails not only adopting a critical stance relative to subjectivity but also cultivating and experimenting with alternative modes (Butler 2004). My analysis of feminist anti-sexual violence protests supports my case for such loosening. Reflecting definitive elements of the sort of parrhesiastic self-relation Foucault elucidates, these protests illustrate that counter-normalizing, counter-humiliating self-transformation occurs in and through an ongoing process of risking becoming otherwise – not only to others and the world, but also to oneself. In short, I argue that counter-normalizing/counter-humiliating self- and broader transformation entails, as Butler puts it, the "risking" of one's own "ontological status" (2004).

"It is not my responsibility," Christine Blasey Ford asserted in her testimony before the Senate, "to determine whether Mr. Kavanaugh deserves to sit on the Supreme Court. My responsibility is to tell you the truth" (U.S. Senate hearings 2018). Ford's experiences make clear that within the context of the systemic sexism and misogyny of gendered power relations, to speak of one's experience of sexual violence and humiliation is to express a subversive truth. When Ford confronted Kavanaugh, she took on the humiliating conditions and treatment to which that confrontation subjected her. She constituted herself in terms of the truth of sexual assault and sexual humiliation, but she did so precisely in ways that turned the humiliation back against its source. This experience would change her, and as the events that unfolded illustrate, her truth-telling generated change more broadly. Foucault's analysis of *parrhēsia* makes clear, and I emphasize throughout this book, that taking on risk always exposes one to uncertainty. Even as her "worst fears" about stepping forward were realized in the harassment she subsequently experienced, even as she anticipated that her "voice would be drowned out by a chorus of powerful [Kavanaugh] supporters," Ford could not ultimately know in advance what would transpire after she accused Kavanaugh or what broader effects – normalizing and counter-normalizing – that accusation and her subsequent, "terrifying" decision to testify before Congress would generate (U.S. Senate hearings 2018). Her experience thus highlights the connection Foucault draws between expression of subversive truths and courage.

Foucault's view that fundamental to counter-normalization is critiquing what appears as most uncritiquable permeates my analysis in this book. His critique of subjectivity and appeal to counter-normalizing modes of self-relation also helped me to make sense of my own experience. I debated for a very long time whether even to mention in these pages that I was raped when I was an undergraduate student, and I remain ambivalent about doing so now. I don't want to be reduced to that identity, nor do I want what I present in this book to be reduced to my experience. Like Ford, I went decades without speaking publicly about having been sexually violated. Like Ford, I ended up doing so because of the Kavanaugh hearings.

I identify with Christine Blasey Ford.[5] We are both academics. We are close to the same age. I grew up in the Washington, D.C., suburbs of Northern Virginia, very close to where she lived in Maryland. Although I attended public schools, the parties she and others of Kavanaugh's peers described closely resemble those that I and my friends were throwing and attending in high school; her experience with Kavanaugh at one of those parties is all too familiar as well. I can also relate to the reasons for Ford's decades-long public silence. In her opening statement to the Senate Judiciary Committee, Ford remarked that she could never have told her parents she was at a party with boys where no parents were home and alcohol was being consumed; the reduction of rape and sexual assault to mere effects of alcohol consumption, as well as the victim-blaming such reduction reflects and the self-blame it (re)asserts, were just as if not more prevalent when Ford and I were young women. After I was raped, I told a few friends about what had happened to me. I don't recall exactly what I said, but I know I didn't say I had been raped because I didn't think I had been. Rather, I blamed myself for getting into a situation in which something like what happened could have. I do, however, recall that my friends' responses pretty much validated my own interpretation of events: "If you hadn't been drinking, you would not have gotten into a car with people you didn't know. And if you had not gotten into that car, you would not have been in a position to have been taken advantage of." I inevitably felt worse after hearing them. So I stopped talking about it.

Doing feminist scholarship confronted me with the reality that what I had experienced was sexual violence. And yet, prevailing feminist ways of framing that experience didn't work for me. I came to see that I was seeking a way of expressing my experience, and my relationship to that experience, that didn't reduce me to it. The concepts of both victim and survivor seemed to me to do that; albeit in different ways, both modes of meaning-making and identification ultimately kept sexual violation central to who I was.[6] I sought to make sense of violation and have it acknowledged as a harm in decentering ways, to understand and relate to it in ways that loosened my attachment to it and, in doing so, facilitated a process of (self) transformative becoming other than. Ambivalence about exposing myself to the uncertainty onto which my disclosure opens is over-ridden by a Foucauldian conviction that without risking uncertainty relative to oneself and more broadly, change is impossible.

In a recent TED talk, Tarana Burke, founder of MeToo and #MeToo, recites a litany of recent events, including the Kavanaugh hearings, that have left her feeling "numb" (2018).[7] Numbness, Burke contends, is not an absence of feeling but rather an overwhelming accumulation of feelings. Certainly, I have experienced such an accumulation due to developments in the U.S. during and since the 2016 presidential election, everything I have read in researching and writing this book, and the intellectual and emotional reactions those developments and texts have generated. The Kavanaugh hearings, however, invoked a particularly intense response on my part – a simultaneous rage and despair that emerged at the moment I read that Kavanaugh had been accused. Because I feared, even as, like Suzanna Danuta Walters, I really, *really* didn't want to be right, that we were headed for a repeat of the Anita Hill-Clarence Thomas hearings. So, when I presented a paper at the National Women's Studies Association conference a few weeks after Kavanaugh's confirmation that analyzed sexual humiliation in terms of that whole debacle and someone asked me, "Why humiliation?", I replied in the way I usually do, saying that humiliation as a key harm of sexual violence against women is undertheorized within philosophy. But I then added, with what I described as "brutal honesty," that when I was raped, humiliation was a pervading and enduring response. For me, the Kavanaugh hearings had made silence impossible. Upon breaking her own long silence, Padma Lakshmi writes: "[W]e all have a lot to lose if we put a time limit on telling the truth about sexual assault and if we hold on to the codes of silence that for generations have allowed men to hurt women with impunity" (2018). At the same time, and as I shall emphasize in what follows, no one should be compelled to speak publicly. Something has to make silence untenable to the point that the risk of speaking out is preferable. No one reaches that point in the same way or after the same length of time.

My remarks about my own experience show that it is not irrelevant to what I write in this book; at the same time, that experience should not be construed as the book's motivation. Rather, reading Foucault's late work and bringing it into conversation with feminist theory led to the emergence of philosophical questions concerning sexual violence, sexual humiliation, and the countering of both that in turn related back to my own circumstances. It is those broader questions that are taken up within the analysis that follows.

Chapter 1, "You Can't Critique the Subject," clears the way for analysis in subsequent chapters of the interconnection of subjectivity with (sexual) humiliation, and the exploration of alternative, counter-normalizing/counter-humiliating modes of self-relation. I show, contra the assertion reflected in the chapter's title, that in addition to that of Foucault, the work of Friedrich Nietzsche and Judith Butler not merely reformulates subjectivity but more fundamentally unsettles its uncritical acceptance as a necessary ground for intelligibility and meaningful action. All three thinkers, moreover, are motivated by concerns about subjectivity's function as a harmful mode of self-relation. The chapter fully elaborates the normalizing character of subjectivity by turning to Foucault's 1980 and 1982 courses, *On the Government of the Living* and *The Hermeneutics of the Subject*. The genealogy he provides shows that subjectivity is grounded in, remains bound up with, and consequently reasserts definitive characteristics of the early Christian relation of self to self. Forged by way of the practices of baptism, penance, and (especially) confession, this mode of self-relation possesses the normalizing characteristics of obedience, conformity, individuation, and internalization; ultimately, it requires and thus reasserts self-renunciation. Foucault also shows that despite its harmful effects and lack of ontological necessity, human beings have forged deep attachments to subjectivity as a mode of self-relation. I conclude the chapter by discussing Butler's point that loosening these attachments is fraught in part because it entails risking one's own ontological status and therefore one's intelligibility. I acknowledge that such loosening is particularly difficult from a feminist perspective but nonetheless contend that the risk it entails facilitates rather than undermines feminist efforts toward countering sexual violence and the sexual humiliation such violence inflicts.

Chapter 2, "Subjectivity, Sexual Violence, and Sexual Humiliation," provides accounts of both humiliation generally and sexual humiliation more specifically and shows that sexual violence humiliates. Marking a distinction between humiliating conditions and treatment on the one hand and the experience of humiliation on the other, I show that humiliation manifests within the relation of self to self by means of and subsequently intensifies definitive, normalizing features of subjectivity. As a redoubling of that intensification, sexual humiliation generates a deeply damaging relation of self to self that threatens to foreclose victims'/survivors' critical and creative capacities, the very resources upon which they need to draw in order to engage in counter-action. Drawing upon the work of contemporary feminist philosophers, I elucidate the damaging and normalizing character of sexual humiliation through analysis of recent cases of rape and sexual assault. To conclude the chapter, I acknowledge that and explore possible reasons why some victims/survivors of sexual violence do not, at least not initially, experience humiliation. By illustrating the importance for feminism of loosening attachments to subjectivity, this chapter opens onto analysis in subsequent chapters of contemporary forms of feminist anti-sexual violence protest that reflect such loosening and thereby offer insight into alternative modes of self-relation.

Chapter 3, "Speaking Out, Countering Sexual Humiliation, Transforming Oneself," begins by providing an overview of *parrhēsia* (truth-telling) as Foucault presents it in his 1983 Collège de France course, *The Government of Self and Others*. As a sort of counter-confession, *parrhēsia* cultivates a mode of self-relation that directly opposes obedience, conformity, individuation, and internalization, and which is therefore not characterized by self-renunciation. The chapter focuses on what Foucault refers to as judicial *parrhēsia*, a particular form of the broader, verbal practice of political *parrhēsia*; apropos to the current analysis, the paradigmatic example of judicial *parrhēsia* for Foucault entails a woman (Creusa, Ion's mother in Euripides' play, *Ion*) confronting her rapist (the god Apollo). The chapter proceeds by analyzing the feminist significance of particular acts of women's verbal anti-sexual violence protest: legal testimony by thirteen women who were sexually violated by former Oklahoma City police officer Daniel Holtzclaw, the Brown University "Rape List," and #MeToo. I show that these protests reflect definitive characteristics of judicial *parrhēsia*, elucidate their counter-normalizing/counter-humiliating effects, and argue that they can be seen as expressing counter-normalizing/counter-humiliating modes of self-relation. Speaking out opened onto women's experiencing their relationship to truth and hence to themselves in ways that disrupt the internalization and individuation that characterize subjectivity and upon which sexual humiliation hinges. I conclude the chapter by considering what it has cost the speakers in question to loosen their attachments to subjectivity and hence risk their own ontological status.

Chapter 4, "Militant Bodies," turns to ethical *parrhēsia* as Foucault presents it in his 1984 Collège course, *The Courage of Truth*. The "militant" ethical *parrhēsia* of the Cynics upon which Foucault focuses cultivates a mode of embodied existence that overtly and aggressively challenges prevailing norms. Through its "bearing witness" to subversive truths, militant ethical *parrhēsia* generates possibilities for oppositionally transformative ways of constituting, understanding, and relating to oneself, others, and world. Significantly, militant self-transformation occurs through a subversive taking on humiliation that turns it back against and therefore confront its source. The chapter analyzes two forms of feminist anti-sexual violence protest, SlutWalks and Emma Sulkowicz's "Mattress Protest/Carry that Weight," that reflect defining characteristics of militant Cynic ethical *parrhēsia*. Participants in these protests publicly display and thereby assert precisely in its susceptibility to violation an embodied self-relation upon which sexual violence and humiliation have been inflicted. The protests reflect an externalizing taking on of humiliation; they express the truth of victims'/survivors' experiences in ways that do not require them to perpetually constitute and identify themselves in terms of it. I conclude the chapter by discussing the importance of courage for the purposes of cultivating counter-normalization and counter-humiliation both within the self-relation and more broadly, and by asserting that not only courage but militancy more generally open onto articulating alternative conceptualizations of solidarity.

The book's conclusion, "Gestures of Solidarity," explores how the counter-normalizing/counter-humiliating characteristics of and effects generated by the forms of political protest analyzed in Chapters 3 and 4 can be and in fact are being cultivated between individuals within the context of daily life practices. Drawing upon the work of Butler and Maurice Merleau-Ponty, I present gesture as an everyday expression of solidarity. As verbal and embodied expressions, gestures facilitate victims'/survivors' making sense of their experience and meaningfully expressing it within a context of normalization generally and gendered relations of power more specifically. Gestures of solidarity make possible connections that are forged on a shared experience of becoming other to oneself that takes the form of a transformative disclosure, the effects of which cannot be known in advance. These gestures neither merely reflect nor, therefore, merely reproduce existing ways (even feminist ways) of constituting, understanding, and relating either to sexual violence or to victims/survivors. Rather, gestures of solidarity require mutual risk, courage, openness to transformation, and willingness to fail. In short, these gestures and the practices onto which they open confront, (critically) engage, and ultimately affirm rather than disavow the interconnection of self-relation and other/world relations.

The Kavanaugh hearings provide only the most recent illustration of the fact that the specter of failed testimony and subsequent need for ongoing efforts to "transmit meaning" from the experience of sexual violence to "after" continue to haunt victims/survivors (Insana 2009, 14; 17–22).[8] When making sense of the experience of sexual violation and humiliation is itself a struggle; when that violation and humiliation are not recognized as injuries; and when efforts to communicate that injury and struggle are met with general ambivalence as well as particular expressions ranging from doubt to disdain to overt hostility – and, hence, further humiliation – the question of why victims/survivors remain silent for decades expresses profound epistemic ignorance. Within the normalizing, oppressive context that generates these effects, giving expression to that experience can feel not merely like one is trying to convey events that occurred on another planet, but like one is actually inhabiting and speaking from that alien location. This book aims to contribute to and further broaden counter-normalizing and counter-humiliating feminist interventions within and disruptions of gendered relations of power, and in doing so to generate conditions under which practices of freedom and expressions of solidarity flourish.

Notes

1 The title of this chapter references the title of an interview with Foucault, "How Much Does It Cost for Reason to Tell the Truth?," as it appears in *Foucault Live*, an edited collection of interviews he gave between 1961 and 1984. The editors of the collection indicate that the interview was originally published in 1983 under the title, "How Much Does It Cost to Tell the Truth?" (see Foucault 1996).

2 Like Cahill and Brison, in focusing on sexual violence against women by men I am not denying that men are also victims of sexual violence. Moreover, while my work may speak to the experiences of some trans women, the specific conditions for the possibility of sexual violence against trans women, as well as the specific characteristics, prevalence, and effects of such violence, are beyond the scope of the current analysis.

3 Milano tweeted: 'If you've been sexually harassed or assaulted write "me too" as a reply to this tweet.' https://twitter.com/alyssa_milano/status/919659438700670976?lang=en.

4 My focus, as I indicate, is humiliation and sexual humiliation that are externally *imposed* by way of perceptions of subhumanization that result in treatment as if nonhuman. I am not addressing practices such as BDSM where sexual subordination is welcomed.

5 Many women identified with Ford (see Nilsen 2018).

6 Throughout this book, I use the terminology "victim/survivor" when referring to women who have experienced sexual violence. On the one hand, I want to use recognizable, relatable, and accurate terminology. Women who have experienced sexual violence have been victimized and have survived a violent attack. On the other hand, I hope that bringing the two concept together in a way that simultaneously contrasts them contributes a critical element that helps to resist their reductive potential. When describing the condition of women within the context of an act of sexual violence, however, I simply use the term "victim."

7 Milano appropriated Tarana Burke's terminology in her tweet. Burke (as is now widely acknowledged) founded #MeToo. For reasons I discuss in Chapters 3 and 5, I distinguish between the broad phenomenon #MeToo and "Me Too" as the phrase functions within Burke's work at Girls for Gender Equity. In my view, the latter possesses counter-normalizing/counter-humiliating potential, specifically as a gesture of solidarity, whereas I am more ambivalent about #MeToo in this regard. The distinction I mark is therefore not a failure to recognize Burke as #MeToo's founder.

8 I borrow this terminology from Lina Insana in her book, *Arduous Tasks: Primo Levi, Translation, and the Transmission of Holocaust Testimony*. Insana analyzes Levi's efforts to convey meaning "from Auschwitz to after." According to Insana, these efforts were motivated by Levi's deep concern about the failure of survivor testimony, a failure that, she contends, was for him "almost worse than the reality of Auschwitz itself" (17) (see Insana 2009).

1 "You can't critique the subject"

As is the case with much published scholarly work, the ideas that developed into the content of this book were aired publicly for the first time at an academic conference. The question and answer period that followed my presentation did not open with a question, however, but rather with a pointed comment. "You can't critique the subject," a member of the audience flatly stated. Because the subject is a condition for the possibility of intelligibility, this individual asserted, endeavoring to critique it was, on the one hand, simply incoherent. Moreover, insofar as such a critique undermined agency and, therefore, possibilities for resistance, bringing it to bear on the phenomenon of sexual violence against women was particularly problematic. In the face of this dismissive response, remarks from the Introduction to Judith Butler's book, *Bodies that Matter*, came to mind. Repeatedly confronted with the question, "What about the materiality of the body, *Judy?*", Butler writes that she felt like she was being "taken aside" and shown the error of her ways (1993, ix; x; original emphasis). Ultimately, though, I found the response instructive because it reflected the very problem to which I was endeavoring to draw attention: uncritical acceptance of the ontological necessity of subjectivity as a mode of self-relation. From the perspective of my interlocutor, subjectivity might be redefined or reconceptualized but, like the body (according to Butler's critics), its ontological status was unassailable.

This initial and subsequent critical responses to my work, as well as exchanges I've had with scholars who are open to my perspective, have served to clarify, more fully develop, and strengthen – and strengthen my commitment to – the overarching arguments I made in that early conference paper. First, it is possible to critically analyze not only particular formulations of subjectivity, but also and more fundamentally its ontological status, without undermining either intelligibility or possibilities for meaningful action. Second, critical analysis reveals that conceiving of subjectivity as an ontological necessity, in the sense that it functions as the sole condition for the possibility of intelligibility and meaningful action, masks the normalizing relations of power in which subjectivity and its uncritical acceptance are implicated. Such a conceptualization thereby facilitates reproduction and even proliferation of normalization. Third, then, by revealing subjectivity's normalizing character, critical analysis both calls for and opens onto alternative, potentially counter-normalizing modes of three self-reflexive actions that collectively comprise what I refer to throughout this book as the "relation of self to (it)self" or simply the "self-relation": self-constitution, self-understanding, and self-relation. Critical analysis therefore furthers emancipatory ethical and political projects such as the one with which I am concerned here: contributing to and furthering feminist efforts toward countering sexual violence against women and, therefore, the sexual humiliation resulting from this violence. Fourth, and finally, the genealogy of subjectivity Michel Foucault generates in his late work, especially his Collège de France courses, provides such critical analysis and therefore contributes to such projects. The second, third, and fourth arguments obviously hinge upon the first. If subjectivity is an ontological necessity, then as my conference interlocutor implied, setting out to critique it is not merely incoherent but harmful – even "schizophrenic and suicidal," as Jürgen Habermas describes philosophical projects that challenge the necessity of concepts, categories, and principles that function as conditions for the possibility of intelligibility as such (1999, 102).[1]

In addressing these concerns, this chapter clears the way for the analysis of sexual violence and humiliation and their countering that follows in the rest of the book. I show that critique of subjectivity's ontological necessity is possible, has in fact already been performed, and reveals subjectivity to be both a contingent and normalizing mode of self-relation. Such critique, moreover, reveals that despite its lack of ontological necessity, human beings (or at least philosophers) have forged deep attachments to subjectivity that inhibit its thorough unpacking. I conclude by presenting what, in my view, "loosening" these attachments, as Butler puts it, entails and discussing why this loosening is important and difficult, especially within a feminist context.

I

I initially responded to my conference interlocutor's confident assertion that it was impossible (and dangerous) to critique the ontological necessity of subjectivity by exclaiming, "Well, he (meaning Foucault) does it!" But Foucault is not the only and certainly not the first philosopher to have engaged in such a critique. Nietzsche, of course, calls into question the ontological necessity afforded to all "central modernist categories," as well as the will to systematization of reality and experience in which they are implicated (Hatab 2005, 49). "Let us beware," he cautions, "of positing generally and everywhere anything as elegant as the cyclical movements of our neighboring stars; even a glance into the Milky Way raises doubts whether there are not far coarser and more contradictory movements there" (1974, 167–168). Nietzsche's well-known pronouncement that 'there is no "being" behind doing' and description of "'the doer'" as "merely a fiction added to the deed" reflect his view that subjectivity acquires its status as the uncontestable ground for intelligibility and meaningful action primarily through conventions of language (1989a, 45). These conventions, he contends in "On Truth and Lies in a Nonmoral Sense," are a product of human sociality (1979). Nietzsche describes language emerging in response to the need to communicate with and therefore refer to others; at the same time, he also shows that *self*-referentiality is implicit with these interactions. The notion of an "I" and the accompanying notion of "self" that emerge in language allow individuals to experience themselves as distinct and hence distinguish themselves from others: "I" am not "them;" "they" are not "me." Self-referentiality facilitates an experience of (my)self as possessing shared human "attributes," "faculties," and capacities at the same time that, as a "discrete," "enduring," and therefore discernable entity, these attributes, faculties, and capacities manifest in particular ways that are unique to "me" (Hatab 2005, 50).[2] So construed, self-referentiality in turn opens onto the experiences of individuality, internality, and self-awareness in the form of (self)consciousness. Of these three experiences, all of which come to be construed not as modes of self-constitution but rather as reflecting what the "I" simply is, Nietzsche argues that self-consciousness becomes most definitive of what it means to be human and, hence, to be a subject. "One thinks," he writes, "that [consciousness] constitutes the *kernel* of man; what is abiding, eternal, ultimate and most original in him" (1974, 85; original emphasis).

For Nietzsche, subjectivity functions as a mode of self-relation that "protects" us from the uncertainty that characterizes our existence by very effectively reproducing the idea that human beings possess an abiding, eternal, and ultimate "kernel" (Hatab 2005, 50).[3] Human beings experience fear and anxiety in the face of the death of God. Rather than endeavoring to create meaning where it is no longer simply given, we simultaneously turn away from and *impose* certainty on the world through systematizing not only the world itself, but also our experiences of and within it. By assigning causal explanations and reproducing the familiar and the already known, systematization assuages anxiety and fear that even potential uncertainty produces. "The cause-creating drive," Nietzsche writes,

> is . . . conditioned and excited by the feeling of fear. The question "why?" should furnish, if at all possible, not so much the cause for its own sake as a *certain kind of cause* – a soothing, liberating, alleviating cause . . . The new, the unexperienced, the strange is excluded from being a cause.
>
> (Nietzsche 2003, 62)

In sum, then, to perform the dual role of meaning-maker and – guarantor, a subject must possess both self-consciousness and the capacity to serve as the ground for its own intelligibility and action. To perform its more specific role as ethico-political actor or agent, the subject must be reasonable, free-willed, autonomous, and capable of memory (Nietzsche 1989a). As vehicles for the production of meaning and providers of certainty, these attributes, faculties, and capacities facilitate our efforts to eradicate uncertainty and the fear and anxiety it generates; as such, they come to be experienced as merely positive or enabling. Construing and experiencing subjectivity as purely positive and enabling produces a deep attachment to it; as a result, human beings *re*constitute ourselves as subjects to the point where subjectivity acquires its status as an ineluctable mode of being.

And yet, Nietzsche also shows, subjectivity's enabling facets emerge in reaction against uncertainty, the threat of meaninglessness it appears to pose, and the negative emotions it generates. It therefore remains bound up with them. As Butler emphasizes, "external differentiation" – forming a self-relation against what is "not me" – enables "my discreteness and specificity" and thus, even as I disavow it, remains internal to and therefore constitutive of me (2010, 142). On the one hand, then, attachment to subjectivity reproduces and intensifies the negative phenomena and accompanying emotions it is meant to eradicate. On the other hand, as Nietzsche shows in the Second Essay of the *Genealogy*, these ostensibly purely enabling and therefore positive attributes, faculties, and capacities both generate and legitimate harmful effects in their own right. The notion of the subject as free and autonomous leads to the idea that when one acts or fails to act one does so of one's own accord. If actions and failures to act are free and willed, the subject can be held responsible for them and the effects they generate. The concept of responsibility is internalized and reinforced through attributing to us the capacity for memory, which makes the subject accountable not only to others but also to itself. Free will, responsibility, and memory allow determinations of guilt to be made in the face of failures of action and inaction, and punishment to be meted out – either by means of external sanction or internally by means of the experience of "bad conscience" (Nietzsche 1989a).

Nietzsche presents subjectivity as a particular form the self-relation has acquired. A response to, which is at the same time grounded in and reproduces the negative experiences (uncertainty and its possibility) and emotions (fear and anxiety) it is intended to counter, subjectivity is nonetheless construed and experienced as an ontological necessity in the sense of being a condition for the possibility of both intelligibility and agency. Nietzsche shows, moreover, that subjectivity's characteristic and most valued attributes, faculties, and capacities both promote and justify harmful effects in their own right. In light of these revelations, Nietzsche considers *his genealogical critique* to facilitate meaningful action, even as it calls for (and itself engages in) reconceptualization of the nature of such action. Finally, Nietzsche does not deny either that we have a relationship to ourselves or the significance of this relationship relative to our own intelligibility. His conceptualization of self-overcoming opens onto and engages questions concerning how we might constitute, understand, and relate to ourselves differently; how we might reconsider our own ontological attachments; and what a self-relation that doesn't experience itself solely as the singular condition for the possibility of intelligibility and agency might look like.

Consistent with Nietzsche's perspective, Foucault considers subjectivity to be a particular mode of self-relation that emerges as an effect of particular experiences within a particular sociohistorical context. In an interview given not long before his death, Foucault was asked whether he considered subjectivity to be "the condition of possibility of experience." "Absolutely not," he replied (1985, 11). The ancient Greeks, Foucault contends, were concerned with constituting themselves as self-masterful individuals, but this self-constitution (and subsequent self-understanding and self-relation) was not synonymous with subjectivization, the processes by means of which human beings "obtain the constitution of a subject" (12). Subjectivity, Foucault asserts, "is of course only one of the given possibilities of organization of a self-consciousness" (Ibid). Identifying and analyzing other distinct historical modes of self-relation both underscores his critique of subjectivity's ontological necessity and opens onto the idea that alternative modes of self-relation can be cultivated in the present.

Even these brief remarks show that Foucault rejected the view that "man" could "serve as the foundation of his own finitude" (1994, 341). From his perspective, taking subjectivity to be ontologically necessary functions in the service of normalizing power. For Foucault, as is well-established in his own work as well as in secondary literature, power is not possessed or held, either by an individual such as a king or dictator, or by the state or state-run institutions, or even by particular social groups.[4] Rather, power is a complex matrix of different networks of, as Foucault puts it, actions acting upon other actions (1983a, 220).[5] Power relations generate effects, but these effects do not reflect the will of any particular individual, government, institution, or group. In addition to being both "intentional" and "nonsubjective," power relations are ubiquitous, manifesting at both macro- (structural, institutional) and micro- (individual, even "cellular") levels, as well as characteristically unequal (Foucault 1990a, 95).

Where there is no getting outside of power, and no possibility of establishing equality within it, freedom becomes not a state of being but instead an ongoing practice of navigating power relations in ways that modify, expand, and even reverse them. The more extensive and dynamic relations of power are, the more (and the more ways in which) they are open to ongoing critical and creative reconfiguration: a multiplicity of divergent actions generates a proliferation of disparate and diverging effects. Navigating this kind of shifting and changing, "open and fluid," power matrix requires lightness of feet: nimbleness, alertness, inventiveness, and a predilection toward the experimental (Foucault 1980a). It requires the capacities Foucault identifies as refusal, curiosity, and innovation: challenging what is presented as "self-evident;" critically reflecting on our own contemporary reality; and engaging that reality in order to "seek out in our reflection those things that have never been thought or imagined" (Ibid).[6] By consistently expanding, diversifying, and reconfiguring them, such navigation hones the broader critical and creative capacities identified above.

Ultimately, relations of power are characterized by an interconnection of enablement (increased, and in certain senses enhanced attributes, faculties, capacities) and constraint (limited functioning, exercise, and expression of those attributes, faculties, and capacities). It is through, not despite, navigating power relations that enablement may be maximized and constraint minimized. That engaging in the practice of freedom (re)produces the conditions under which it can continue to be practiced helps to explain why, for Foucault, inequality and freedom are not opposed but rather mutually implicate one another. Navigating power relations mitigates against the formation of patterns of inequality that characterize institutional and structural oppression. If such patterns begin to emerge, they can be subverted, redirected, and even deployed – they need not be endlessly reproduced. It is thus through navigating power relations that we are able to participate in shaping the conditions of our existence: our relationships to ourselves, others, and the world.

Normalization fosters conditions under which patterns of inequality may form and become entrenched or static.[7] Normalizing power relations channel critical and creative capacities into a few predictable patterns that (re)generate the same effects – that, in other words, reproduce prevailing norms. Where the same actions repeatedly encounter and act upon one another, reconstructing the same networks within the overall power matrix, they come to be seen and experienced (when they are seen and experienced at all) simply as natural, necessary, "normal" fixtures.[8] Its broad uncritical acceptance and, indeed, desirability (which stem from the myriad ways, obvious and subtle, in which it is inculcated) in turn very effectively sustains the conditions for the reproduction of the normal. Where prevailing conditions are taken as not only necessary but also efficacious, critical and creative capacities contract; moreover, being repeatedly directed toward the same, foreseen ends instrumentalizes those which remain. Human beings become highly adept and efficient at inculcating prevailing relations of power: we energetically direct ourselves toward doing what we already know how to do and reproducing what already exists, all the while taking it to be the sum total of what there is to know, of all that exists, and of all that is good.

In short, normalization produces a context of deep constraint, at the same time that it creates and subsequently masks the conditions under which constraint is experienced as (purely) enabling. If we construe and experience enablement and constraint as distinct and opposite, we cannot effectively navigate power relations in ways that maximize the former and minimize the latter. Neither can we effectively apprehend how failing to grasp the nature and function of normalizing power inures us to its harmful effects, such as structural and institutional oppression. With diminished critical and creative capacities, not only are we less able to participate in shaping conditions of existence, we are more likely to allow it to be done for us; that is, we become predisposed toward complacency and conformity.

Normalization not only makes us flat-footed, it encourages an experience of that flat-footedness as nimbleness.

Foucault analyzes and elucidates the normalizing character of subjectivity in an in-depth genealogy that spans the courses he presented at the Collège de France between 1980 and 1984. He reveals subjectivity to be a deeply constraining mode of constituting, understanding, and relating to ourselves which, through masking its own harmful effects, is experienced as fundamentally and even purely enabling and thus perpetually reproduced. The critique of subjectivity Foucault articulates in these courses resonates with Nietzsche's in two important respects. First, like Nietzsche, he locates subjectivity's definitive enabling aspect in its ostensible ontological necessity; second, he locates subjectivity's origins in the experience of uncertainty and the negative affective responses that experience generates. Foucault begins in 1980 by tracing the coalescing within early Christianity generally and monasticism more specifically of the conditions under which subjectivity acquires its status as ontological necessity and defining characteristics. Foucault advances his argument in 1982 by showing that what are ostensibly the same characteristics manifest in divergent and even opposing ways within the ancient Greek and Greco-Roman relations of self to self and, therefore, that the relation of self to self in these earlier two contexts is not (yet) subjectivity.[9] If the relation of self to self has not always taken the form of subjectivity, then it follows that it need not, and Foucault's illustration of subjectivity as a harmful mode of self-relation further clears the way for his analysis in 1983 and 1984 of alternative, potentially counter-normalizing modes of relating to ourselves. I will draw upon those two courses in Chapters 3 and 4 in order to explore what counter-normalizing modes of the relation of self to self might look like. Following Foucault, the next section of this chapter both illustrates the possibility of and makes a case for that exploration.

II

In his 1980 course, *On the Government of the Living*, Foucault analyzes the Western phenomenon of making a relationship to truth requisite for forming a relationship to oneself, as well as how this formation is implicated in relations of power. With respect to subjectivity specifically, Foucault raises the following questions relative to the general course theme:

> Why and how does the exercise of power in our society, the exercise of power as government of men, demand not only acts of obedience and submission, but truth acts in which individuals who are subjects in the power relationship are also subjects as actors, spectator witnesses, or objects in manifestation of truth procedures? Why in this great system of relations of power has a regime of truth developed indexed to subjectivity?

> (2014, 82)

Foucault shows in his 1982 course, *The Hermeneutics of the Subject*, that historico-cultural conditions provide the broader normative framework within which the self-relation/truth/power matrix forms and gets configured; he focuses on how the "cultural phenomenon" of care of the self shapes the self-relation. In its most general sense, care of the self refers to "a way of being," "standpoint," or "attitude" (Foucault 2005, 10–11). To care for oneself is to cultivate a relationship – "the right kind" of relationship – to oneself. Self-cultivation was performed by way of various sets of "practices" and "forms of reflection" (for example, meditation, memorization of the past, examination of conscience, self-writing, diet, and exercise) that collectively Foucault refers to as "technologies of the self" (11). Consistent with the theme of the 1980 course, Foucault is particularly interested in a technology of the self he refers to as "conversion," the transformative process through which a (self)relationship in, through, and to the truth was forged. In Classical and Hellenistic Greece, late Antiquity, and early Christianity, the self-relation was not considered to and subsequently did not experience itself as having a *prima facie* relationship to truth. Where one "does not have right of access to the truth," Foucault explains, one must "be changed, transformed, shifted, and become, to some extent and up to a certain point, other than himself" (15). In each of the historico-cultural contexts Foucault considers, individuals were guided or directed in how to care for themselves, and, hence, through the process of conversion more specifically, by another person – a master to whom they subordinated themselves. "[T]here is no care of the self," he writes, "without the presence of a master" (58).

Foucault's 1980 and 1982 courses identify fundamental differences separating early Christian conversion from its predecessors, deviations and oppositions that lay the ground for subjectivity's coalescence. A first point of difference concerns the role obedience plays in establishing a relationship to oneself that is simultaneously a relationship to the truth. In ancient Greece and late Antiquity, conversion aims to achieve the autonomy of the individual undergoing it; obedience to the master is therefore temporary. In 1982, Foucault analyzes the *Alcibiades* in order to show that Socrates, the master, guides the subordinate and therefore obedient Alcibiades through the transformative process that will equip him to care for himself. Correct care of himself will enable Alcibiades to properly care for others and, ultimately, to participate in governing the city of Athens.[10]

Greco-Roman care of the self and conversion were not exclusive to young men who, like Alcibiades, were entering public and political life. Foucault explains that the Stoics, for example, undertook transformative work on themselves for its own sake. Insofar as care of others or governance of the state were simply its side effects, Stoic men of all ages engaged in care of the self throughout the entire course of their lives (Foucault 2005, 206–207). The perpetual nature of care of the self did not mean, however, that its practitioners existed in a permanent state of obedience. Stoic care of the self was "integrated within, mixed up, and intertwined with a whole network of different social relations in which mastership in the strict sense still exists, but in which there are also many other possible forms of relationships" (206). One of the social relations Foucault considers is friendship. At various points during their lives, friends would guide one another, with the roles of master and subordinate being broadly construed as well as reversible.[11]

A second point of difference concerns the precise nature of the self-transformation that occurs in conversion. In both ancient and Greco-Roman contexts, conversion is characterized by a series of self-reflexive turning movements.[12] "It is towards ourselves, towards the center of ourselves," Foucault explains, "that we must fix our aim. And the movement we must make must be to turn back to this center of ourselves in order to immobilize ourselves there . . ." (2005, 207). The series of turns that comprises ancient Greek conversion in the specific form of the Platonic *epistrophē* reflects the interconnection of care of the self with the (in some sense parallel, in some sense competing) principle "know thyself." In Platonic care of the self, one gains "access to truth" by way of knowledge in general, and knowledge of one's own divine nature or soul more specifically. The *epistrophē*, as Foucault describes it, involves first a "turning away from appearances;" second, a "turning around toward oneself" so that one may care for oneself; and, third, a (re)turn – a "recollecting" or recalling of one's true self or "ontological homeland" (209). While Greco-Roman conversion also entails a series of self-reflexive turnings, it focuses on *askēsis* – exercise, practice, and training – rather than knowledge. This movement of the self relative to itself is variously described as "consider[ing] yourself," "observ[ing] yourself," "turning your back on yourself," and "applying your mind to the self" (225; 213). Once again taking the Stoics as an example, the series of turns does not, as in the *epistrophē*, move one from "the world below to the world above" (210). Rather, conversion occurs, and hence truth is accessed, within "the immanence of" the material world (Ibid). One turns away and is thus liberated "from what we do not control so as finally to arrive at what we can control" and thus establishes an "adequate" relation to oneself (Ibid).

The third and final difference between ancient and Greco-Roman conversion, on the one hand, and early Christian conversion, on the other, is apparent in which party, master or subordinate, shoulders "the obligations of truth" (Foucault 2005, 408). Although in ancient and Greco-Roman conversion the subordinate gains access to it, truth is ultimately the concern of the master, the one who "transmits" it (Ibid). Because the master is responsible for the subordinate's transformation, ensuring access to truth and the correct relation of self to self it facilitates "falls essentially" to him as "the guide, or the friend . . . the person who gives advice" (Ibid).

That early Christian conversion breaks with and even opposes its predecessors on each of these points stems from a more fundamental difference in the structure of the relation of self to self in early Christianity. Foucault identifies two early Christian regimes of truth, in tension but nonetheless interconnected.[13] Within the first such regime, truth was construed in terms of acts of faith. Such acts entailed acceptance of, "adherence to," and subsequently a "profession of faith" which was made on the basis of "an inviolable and revealed truth" (i.e., institutionalized religious doctrine, texts, teachings, etc.) (Foucault 2014, 84). Foucault's interest lies primarily in the second regime of truth: acts of confession. These acts obligated individuals to "have a continuous relationship with themselves" that entailed "discovering," "endlessly exploring," and ultimately "manifesting" the "deep secrets within themselves, secrets that elude them" (83; 103). Expressing these elusive parts of oneself, Foucault explains, was considered a manifestation of truth – the truth, that is, of an individual's refutation of evil; acts of confession were in this sense considered to be redemptive for the individuals who engaged in them (103).

The idea that individuals possess an internal dimension that is opaque to them marks a significant departure from ancient Greek and Greco-Roman conceptualizations of the relation of self to self. Constituting one's relationship to oneself, and therefore to the truth, by way of one's "elusive" or hidden aspects introduces an element of inherent uncertainty into the self-relation that paves the way for the emergence, transcendence, and consolidation of subjectivity. An enabling aspect of the early Christian relation of self to self is the capacity to perform the work of self-decipherment required to reveal its own hidden components. At the same time, as a condition for the possibility of this decipherment, the (constraining) uncertainty that characterizes the self-relation remains bound up with it, thereby reproducing and sustaining doubts as to whether that work has been (or can be) performed sufficiently. This interconnection of uncertainty with that which aims to eradicate it clarifies Foucault's description of early Christian self-examination as "endless": the more assiduously one seeks to uncover what was hidden, the more one reproduces one's relation to oneself in terms of concealment and, hence, uncertainty.

Foucault's analysis of early Christian conversion (*metanoia*) elucidates the ambivalent relationship to truth that characterizes a relation of self to self constituted in terms of uncertainty relative to itself. Each of the three practices of conversion Foucault considers – baptism, canonical penance, and spiritual direction – aims to definitively establish a permanent relation of self-to-self in terms of truth. He shows, however, that each practice reproduces and even intensifies self-reflexive uncertainty. This simultaneous action of countering and reproducing uncertainty elucidates *metanoia*'s fundamental difference from ancient and Greco-Roman conversion. First, obedience is a permanent fixture in *metanoia*; second, *metanoia* entails not a series of turnings of the self relative to itself, but rather a severing of the self from itself. Making manifest one's truth through expelling or eradicating a simultaneously hidden and objectionable part of oneself, according to Foucault, is an "upheaval," a single, sudden transition from one form of existence to another: "death to life," "mortality to immortality," "darkness to light," "the reign of the devil to that of God" (2005, 211). *Metanoia* entails a "radical change of thought and mind" that takes the more specific form of a self-renunciation (250). Third, as is already apparent, *metanoia* expresses or makes manifest the truth; it is not a process aimed at providing access to it. Moreover, in *metanoia* truth is the concern of individuals undergoing conversion. It is their responsibility, not that of the one guiding them, to bring forth (their) truth, the truth of themselves.

Foucault presents baptism as originally retaining elements of acts of faith. Receiving education in church teachings provided access to truth that culminated with the "illuminating" and purifying water ritual (Foucault 2014, 106). With Tertullian's introduction of the doctrine of original sin at the beginning of the third century, however, the "relationship between truth and purification is inverted," and baptism becomes fully an act of confession.[14] If sin is part of the nature of human beings and therefore internal, the self-decipherment associated with acts of confession must precede baptism: "[i]t is purification . . . that must lead to the truth" (118). Self-decipherment purifies by both rooting out the source of sin, which Tertullian identifies as the existence of Satan within the soul, and making manifest the truth of its expulsion. Baptism's purifying effect was complicated by the fact that Satan, Tertullian believed, could anticipate his own impending expulsion and accordingly "redouble" his efforts. Those who underwent baptism were thus simultaneously purified and imperiled. If "[t]he more Christian one is the more the devil rages," then this peril remained and potentially intensified after baptism (125). The Christian was never out of danger.

This interconnection of purification and danger reflects the interconnection of certainty and uncertainty. Christians must believe the religious teaching that their souls will actually be transformed, that Satan will be expelled, through the ritual of baptism. At the same time, the baptismal transformation not only ensures that they are never completely out of reach of Satan's influence, it also encourages him to more vigorously pursue them. That Satan takes hold internally, within an individual's soul, means that baptized, purified Christians "must never abandon fear," they must exercise "constant anxiety" relative to their own relationship to themselves (Foucault 2014, 126; 127). There "can be no uncertainty . . . that the truth really has been revealed in Scripture," Foucault contends. "But, on the other hand . . . one must never be certain that one is absolutely pure . . . If one wants to have faith, one must never be certain about what one is oneself" (127).

Whereas baptism takes the form of a ritualized act, canonical penance was a status – a long-term, "all-encompassing status" (Foucault 2014, 195).[15] Foucault shows that canonical penance emerged in response to the question of what to do about "relapsed" individuals, heretics who had destroyed the relationship to the truth established by baptism. This "second penance" was determined to be the part of baptism that could be repeated – but only once – in order to restore the soul to its pure state so individuals could rejoin the Christian faith. Penance required individuals to perform transformative work on themselves through which the state of their souls and hence the (elusive) truth of their repentance was made manifest (194). Unlike in baptism, that work was not preparatory. It was precisely through the "reflexive acts" of penance, according to Foucault, that the individual became "operator of the manifestation of his own truth" – specifically, his own truth "as sinner" (198). Because the authenticity of their expression of themselves as sinners, their repentance and, hence, the state of their souls had to be judged by members of the community, the self-"showing" or self-"exposure" that occurred in canonical penance was necessarily public. *Exomologesis*, the "acts and procedures" through which the person doing penance was "invite[d], exhort[ed], or constrain[ed] to show his own truth," entailed practices such as public wearing of "sack clothes," covering the head in ashes, and fasting (201; 1980b).[16] In short, the truth of who one was became manifest by way of acts of self-humiliation. It is this "reproduction of martyrdom" exemplified in *exomologesis*, Foucault argues, that "affirms" and thereby conveys the authenticity of the penitent's self-transformation, "of the rupture with one's self, with one's past, with the world, and with all previous life" (1980b).

Canonical penance and *exomologesis* intensify the interconnection of certainty and uncertainty that acts of confession introduce into the relation of self to self. Foucault points out that the need for and very idea of a second penance undermines the notion that baptism permanently expelled Satan from the soul. Ambivalence relative to certainty and uncertainty is also apparent in the idea that canonical penance, itself a repetition of an ostensibly singular act, was simultaneously a long-term status and itself singular – Foucault's observes that canonical penance takes the paradoxical form of "[a]n unrepeatable repetition of something that . . . cannot be repeatable" (2014, 194). Finally, and most fundamentally, the penitent expresses the truth of who he or she is, a sinner, through acts that undermine that truth by expressing repentance of sin. "I am all the less a sinner," Foucault explains, "when I affirm that I am a sinner" (215). Penance thus performs a simultaneous manifestation and erasure "of what one is" (214).

The simultaneity of certainty and uncertainty, self-assertion, and self-renunciation that characterizes the relation of self to self in baptism and canonical penance crystallizes in the practice of spiritual direction. Monastic spiritual direction, Foucault explains, adopted ancient and Greco-Roman philosophical practices of self-examination, including examination of conscience.[17] These practices were seen as enhancing the self-decipherment required to drive out Satan and thus furthering monasticism's aim of engaging in work that aspired toward attainment of a "life of perfection" (Foucault 2014, 260).[18] As part of a broader program of spiritual direction, self-examination was overseen by another person. Like that which occurs in ancient and Greco-Roman care of the self, then, monastic self-examination requires subordination and is characterized by obedience. Because self-examination is a fixture of monastic life, however, obedience becomes permanent rather than a temporary means to achieving autonomy. Indeed, Foucault observes that in monasticism cultivation of obedience is an end in itself, a "state" to be cultivated by novices and monks alike (268).

Where permanent and ubiquitous obedience characterizes one's relationship to oneself, the role of a spiritual director bears no resemblance to that of a master responsible for conveying and providing access to (self)knowledge and truth. The monastic spiritual advisor's role was simply to give and enforce orders (relative to both novices and to himself) whatever they might be. Foucault notes that "uneducated," coarse monks regularly served as spiritual directors, and he provides examples of absurd orders that novices were made to follow (2014, 269). Ultimately, the objective of spiritual direction is to produce "a state of obedience so permanent and definitive that it subsists even where there is not exactly anyone that one has to obey and even before anyone has formulated an order" (270). One achieves such a state, Foucault argues, not by renouncing one's will as such, but rather through permanently willing the will of the other. In spiritual direction, the humiliation and self-renunciation that characterize penance are generated through cultivating obedience.

Unlike in ancient Greece and late Antiquity, in monasticism permanent obedience is not an impediment to truth. Rather, truth is made manifest precisely in and through obedience and, paradoxically, this manifestation is facilitated by the very aspect of self-examination that appears to inhibit it. Foucault explains that because the sum total of the transformative work of monasticism was *contemplation* of God, a monk's thoughts were identified as the key potential entry point for Satan (2014, 295–298). A monk could know the content of his thoughts; what eluded or was hidden from him was their origin – whether they came from God or the devil. This lack of *discretio* (discernment or "discrimination") relative to himself could, however, be overcome through telling his thoughts to another person – through, that is, coupling the monastic will to obey with an obligation to speak.

A metaphor from John Cassian, in Foucault's view, most effectively illustrates how verbalization in the specific form of confession produces (self) discrimination. For Cassian, the dynamics of confession are analogous to those of a money changer, an individual who "checks the metal of the coin, who checks its nature, its purity, and also the image stamped on it" – in short, who confirms its origin (Foucault 2014, 301). If the coins represent a monk's thoughts, those originating with and thus bearing the mark of Satan could be distinguished based on their "incompatibility with," and therefore resistance to, being brought out into the light – externalized by means of speech (Foucault 1980b). The most difficult thoughts to verbalize, in other words, were the ones most in need of being expunged. "If I cannot say what I think," Foucault elaborates, "it is because what I am thinking is not of good quality" (2014, 305). By identifying the origin of thoughts, verbalization through confession separates the pure from the impure; like an "exorcism," moreover, it facilitates expulsion of the latter (306). A simultaneous obligation to submit and to speak produces the truth not by accounting for "what is taking place in myself," as was the case in ancient Greece and late Antiquity but, more fundamentally, by "revealing something in me that I could not know and that becomes known through [the] work of self-exploration" (308).

Baptism, canonical penance, and spiritual direction all diverge from ancient and Greco-Roman conversion on the three points identified earlier. Each early Christian/monastic practice requires self-examination and decipherment, which makes obedience a state rather than a temporary condition. All three practices entail a breaking of the self with itself rather than a series of self-reflexive turnings, such that the truth of the self is made manifest through its renunciation of itself. Finally, truth is the concern of the one undergoing conversion, the external expression of the truth of their radical transformation. Still, some ambiguity characterizes baptism and canonical penance. Baptism was said to provide salvation, which implies a definitive separation from sin, yet whether it could be repeated and if so in what way and how frequently was questioned. While penance was determined to be unrepeatable, the self-renunciation it required as an expression of the truth of the self was long-term but not permanent. Confession within the context of spiritual direction removes this ambiguity. The dynamic nature of thoughts required their "perpetual and exhaustive" verbalization – probing the deepest recesses of one's self and speaking aloud what one found (Foucault 2014). Verbalization as confession solves the problem of *discretio*, but it does so by establishing obedience – the *total and continual* renunciation of the self's "own wishes" in which it "substitut[es] another's will for its own" – as the singular condition for the manifestation of its truth (309). "It is because I must renounce myself that I must produce the truth of myself," Foucault asserts. "And I produce the truth of myself only because I am working at this renunciation of myself" (Ibid). By establishing a relation of self to self that effectively traps individuals in a cycle of simultaneous self-assertion and self-negation, Foucault observes, early Christianity creates "[o]ne of the greatest problems of Western culture" (1980b). He identifies in the centuries that follow a "deep desire" in the West to find a way "to substitute the positive figure of man for the sacrifice which was, for Christianity, the condition of opening the self as a field of indefinite interpretation" (Ibid).

The Cartesian "reversal" in which a "malicious" and deceptive internal demon becomes a definitive and fundamental source of certainty ostensibly satisfies this desire. (Foucault 2014, 303). In producing an "I am not mistaken" from an "I can always be deceived," Descartes appears to release Western humanity from the perpetual uncertainty and accompanying fear and anxiety that undermines the possibility of a "positive" relation of self to self whose intelligibility does not demand its own continual negation

(Ibid). In monasticism, the omnipresent possibility of deceit meant one could never be certain relative to oneself and therefore had to perpetually speak. For Descartes, as Foucault sees it, that very possibility allows one to know with certainty.

As Foucault notes in 1982, Descartes posits a relation of self to self that locates its own certainty within itself. This is a mode of self-relation that therefore need not undergo transformation in order to have a relationship to the truth; it "only has to be what [it] is . . . to have access in knowledge to the truth that is open to [it] through [its] own structure" (Foucault 2005, 190).[19] This "Cartesian moment" thus marks the emergence of subjectivity, a mode of self-relation that functions as the condition for the possibility of its own intelligibility and agency. Foucault's genealogy of subjectivity makes clear, however, that this is not a moment of unmitigated triumph over uncertainty. Descartes does not eradicate the structure of a self-relation containing an internal element that eludes it; he simply makes that hidden element a source of certainty in its elusiveness. In essence, Foucault sees Descartes retaining but recasting in a positive light the basic hermeneutical structure of the early Christian relation of self to self. The brilliance of this move is found in the fact that the form subjectivity takes as a producer and guarantor of certainty – as, that is, an ontological necessity – effectively masks the fact of its emergence within a specific sociohistorical context as a reactive and defensive response against the uncertainty it ostensibly overcomes. This masking allows subjectivity's enabling attributes, faculties, and capacities to be taken as its sum total, which in turn disavows not only the negative emotions in which it is grounded, but also the perpetual, obedient production of self-negation it inherits from the early Christian relation of self to self.

Descartes appears to save the "hermeneutics of the self" through uncoupling it from self-reflexive uncertainty and self-renunciation; he appears to accomplish the definitive break within the relation of self to self that baptism, canonical penance, and the confession of spiritual direction could not. Following Nietzsche and consistent with Butler, however, Foucault's work reflects the perspective that the masked and disavowed remain constitutive of that which comes into existence at their expense. Visibility in the form of intelligibility remains bound up with concealment and disavowal, ontological necessity with obedience in the form of perpetual self-renunciation. In subjectivity, the internal, hidden, and elusive continue to function as the condition for the possibility of the manifestation of truth. Also retained, then, is the simultaneous obligation to obey and to speak which, Foucault argues, remains "one of the major driving forces in the organization of subjectivity and truth relationships in the modern West" (2014, 311). This retention ensures reproduction of the truth of the self in discourse and, therefore, reproduction of subjectivity.

As a mode of self-relation, subjectivity intensifies self-reflexive uncertainty and therefore the cycle of self-assertion and -renunciation. Masking and disavowal make critique appear at best unnecessary and at worst destructive. To the extent that subjectivity continues to be considered what we are and must be, on the one hand, and as the sole mechanism for intelligibility and agency, on the other, over time we become increasingly efficient at constituting, understanding, and relating to ourselves exclusively as subjects. We therefore remain in a cycle of self-assertion and self-negation where increasingly more effective enactment of our own subjugation is experienced as emancipatory. In short, subjectivity emerges from, is enabled by, and thus remains bound to constraint. Its uncritical repetition reproduces relations of power in which constraint is asserted at the expense of enablement. It is a normalizing mode of relation of self to self.

III

Judith Butler's critique of subjectivity resonates with those of Nietzsche and Foucault. One of the strongest resonances is found in her account of the normative cognitive process she refers to as "framing." As a mode of meaning-making, framing first establishes "schemas of intelligibility," which determine domains of the knowable (Butler 2010, 5). Within those domains, "historically articulated and enforced" normative structures of recognizability both "enable" and provide the context within which recognition occurs (Ibid). Finally, then, recognition simultaneously reflects and grants full ontological, epistemological, and moral consideration (Ibid). Moving from intelligibility to recognition "delimits" and thus reduces one's conceptual field in the sense that not everyone/thing intelligible registers within a framework of recognizability, and not everyone/thing that is recognizable is recognized. Framing is, therefore, normalizing; it produces an experience of reality as given and necessary and in doing so conceals its own mechanisms of production and effects of power – the fact that some fail to (fully) register within a frame of recognition and are thus denied (full) ontological, epistemological, or moral consideration. "Some subjects," Butler writes, appear as '"recognizable" persons,' whereas "others [are] decidedly more difficult to recognize" (2010, 6).

As a condition for the possibility of intelligibility, the 'presumptive "ground" of any normative theory, subjectivity points to the existence of a set of uninterrogated, meta-level normative assumptions that themselves inform the production of a frame (Butler 2010, 138). Butler undertakes this interrogation in order to make apparent and in doing so disrupt "the differential of power" that simultaneously facilitates recognition by producing the subject and masks subjectivity's implication in failures and refusals of recognition (Ibid). Her overarching point here is that the concept of "the subject," which seems to function as a necessary condition for any normative argument or claim, is itself the product of framing; moreover, and consistent with Nietzsche and Foucault, Butler sees the "desire for epistemological certainty and certain judgment" underpinning the rearticulation of prevailing normative frameworks and normalizing relations of power (2010, 150).

The fact that Butler retains the "language of the subject" in the face of her own thorough and compelling undermining of its ontological necessity – not only in *Frames of War* but throughout her work as well – illustrates the depth of feminist attachment to subjectivity (2010, 140). Given that feminists appeal to subjectivity on not only ontological but also political grounds, the depth of feminist attachment to it is hardly surprising. Subjectivity appears all the more necessary as a mode of intelligibility if one sees oneself having been intentionally denied it in the service of one's own subjugation; as Butler shows, recognition is implicated in relations of power. The view that because it affords recognition, subjectivity is necessary for women's emancipation is reflected in early feminist critiques of Foucault's work. A paradigmatic expression of this perspective appears in Nancy Hartsock's contribution, "Foucault on Power: A Theory for Women," to the 1990 volume, *Feminism/Postmodernism*. According to Hartsock, in critiquing subjectivity, Foucault effectively deprives women of a status they have never had the privilege of experiencing and thereby reinscribes their subordination and oppression. "Why is it," Hartsock asks,

> that just at the moment when so many of us who have been silenced begin to demand the right to name ourselves, to act as subjects rather than objects of history, that just then the concept of subjecthood becomes problematic?

> (1990, 163)

Hartsock sees Foucault undermining women's capacity for agency, including and perhaps most importantly the ability to self-define. While there are certainly contemporary feminist scholars who share Hartsock's perspective, much feminist scholarship (including, as I have noted, Butler's own) reflects more closely Susan Hekman's view, voiced at around the same time as Hartsock's, that Foucault reconceptualizes (as well as facilitates reconceptualization of) but does not jettison subjectivity. Hekman argues that Foucault's work is consistent with feminist critiques of modern Western subjectivity as a reflection of, which in turn reproduces, privileged white male idealization of a disembodied, autonomous (i.e., self-contained), rational (i.e., devoid of emotion) agent. "One of the major innovations of Foucault's approach," Hekman writes, "is his redefinition of the subject and, hence, identity" (1996, 3).

I think the views of Foucault's work expressed by Hartsock and Hekman hold appeal because, in quite different ways of course, both affirm feminist attachment to subjectivity. Hartsock reasserts feminist valuing of subjectivity by rejecting Foucault's critique as hostile to feminism; Hekman reasserts feminist valuing of subjectivity by embracing Foucault's critique as consistent with it. As I have made clear in this chapter, however, Foucault's critique of subjectivity is more nuanced and complex than a simple rejection and more fundamental than a reconceptualization.

In an analysis of Foucault's late work, Butler acknowledges the deep "attachment" we as human beings have to "categories that guarantee social existence" (2004, 191). Given that our very intelligibility hinges on such categories, Butler further acknowledges that the task of critiquing, "loosening," and even letting go of such attachments is neither easy nor simple: it requires that we call into question the terms that allow us to make sense of ourselves – our own attachment to our very selves. Loosening attachments is an undertaking that "risk[s] the suspension of one's own ontological status" (192). This is precisely what I am endeavoring to do in this book. What I have presented in this chapter illustrates that loosening attachments to subjectivity is possible, as well as why it is needed; subsequent chapters will elaborate the latter assertion relative to feminism in pointed ways.

Loosening attachments to subjectivity as I conceive of it entails understanding our own relationship to ourselves as a product of framing and endeavoring to work out and deal with the implications. Posed in Butler's terms, loosening attachment to subjectivity entails raising and pursuing questions concerning the kinds of normative assumptions that inform meta-level frames of recognition which situate subjectivity as a necessary component of any schema of intelligibility. It entails endeavoring to articulate and critically analyze the relations of power that present "the subject" as the only "eligible," recognizable way of constituting, understanding, and relating to ourselves, and which thereby establish it as the 'presumptive "ground" of normative debate' (Butler 2010, 138). Loosening attachments to subjectivity also entails, therefore, treating it as a mode of self-relation that is just as much an effect of power, just as much "made," just as much relying upon for its own intelligibility that which it renders unintelligible, as any of its particular manifestations – the cultural subject, the sexual subject, the religious subject (141). Within a context where subjectivity continues to function as a mode of intelligibility, undertaking such a project will be experienced as undermining one's own ontological status. It will feel strange, even alarming. "The task will be," Butler writes,

> to consider . . . threat and disruption not as a permanent contestation of social norms condemned to a pathos of perpetual failure, but rather as a critical resource in the struggle to rearticulate the very terms of symbolic legitimacy and intelligibility.
>
> (1993, 3)

Which brings us back around to Nietzsche and the death of God. The demise of established meaning, Nietzsche makes clear, is not the demise of meaning as such. He acknowledges how unsettling it is, at least initially, to call into question what appear to be not only necessary but also the most positive fixtures of our existence. Because it appears impossible or nonsensical, doing so induces an experience of "vertigo" from which one fears it will be impossible to escape (Nietzsche 1989a, 20). And yet, he contends, pressing forward with such critique opens onto "a new possibility . . . a new demand" (Ibid). This possibility and demand, for him and for Foucault, are one and the same: the exercise of our critical and creative capacities in order to identify, analyze, and counter harmful practices and through doing so to cultivate a meaningful existence, a livable life. Defending his work against charges that positing power and freedom as interconnected destroyed agency, resistance, and therefore freedom itself, Foucault gave the now familiar explanation that in arguing against an outside to power he was not saying "that everything is bad, but that everything is dangerous" (1983b, 231). I believe Foucault, like Nietzsche, saw as most dangerous, and therefore in most need of critical interrogation, precisely those norms that we are told we need not, cannot, or dare not critique.

"The only ethics you can have with regard to the exercise of power," Foucault once said, "is the freedom of others" (1980a). Exercise of our critical and creative capacities is, then, not the sum total of freedom; its exercise also involves identifying and cultivating conditions under which we are able to develop and exercise those capacities and which enable others to do the same. Where critical and creative capacities are understood in terms of refusal, curiosity, and innovation, part of what needs to be refused, analyzed, and countered is the impulse to tell others what to do, as well as to be provided with unequivocal direction. Foucault emphatically refuses to do the former, and he asks why people desire the latter; as I shall show in the next chapter, both impulses are implicated in normalizing power.

Consistent with Nietzsche and Foucault, as well as with the work of Butler and many of the other feminist thinkers to whose work I appeal in this book, my aim is to both enact and foster refusal, curiosity, and innovation. While I do identify and analyze particular forms of feminist practice within which I identify counter-normalizing potential, I do not provide prescriptive accounts of a meaningful existence or a livable life. Nor, as should be very clear at this point, do I present an alternative to subjectivity. When I refer to a "self-relation" throughout this book, I am acknowledging with Nietzsche and Foucault that as human beings within a modern context we do constitute, understand, and relate to ourselves – we have a relationship to ourselves. I endeavor to leave open to the extent possible what that relationship looks like in order to facilitate thinking about multiple modes of self-relation that do not reproduce and, indeed, that counter normalization. As Butler puts it, without an attachment to ourselves "we cannot be" (2004, 191). I want to explore how, through loosening our attachment *to subjectivity*, we can reimagine and therefore experience our attachment *to ourselves* in counter-normalizing ways. "No aspect of reality," Foucault reminds us, "should be allowed to become a definitive and inhuman law" (1980a).

Feminists continue to invoke subjectivity, in my view, for the reasons I have already noted: on the one hand, subjectivity appears as an ontological necessity that can be reformulated but not fundamentally called into question; on the other, it appears as a necessary condition for the possibility of women's freedom. The latter reason, in particular, is not to be taken lightly. Within a context where, as contemporary reality makes painfully clear and as I shall discuss in the chapters that follow, women's ontological status and freedom are already curtailed, risking them appears to exacerbate our invisibility and deepen our oppression. Part of what makes normalization so pernicious, however, is the degree to which perpetual reproduction of prevailing conditions such that they become experienced as not merely familiar but both given and fixed, convinces us that we (at least possess the capacity to) understand "the way things are" sufficiently to develop and uncritically rely upon *the same ways* of making sense of the world, including identifying, analyzing, and countering harmful practices such as oppression and injustice. Normalization, in other words, fosters complacency and conformity even in our efforts toward counter-normalization, as such efforts manifest both individually (that is, with respect to the relation we have to ourselves) and more broadly (with respect to the relations we have to others and the world). This chapter has made a general case for why counter-normalization relative to our relationship to ourselves is important both broadly and from a feminist perspective. In analyzing ways in which subjectivity as a mode of self-relation is implicated in (re)producing sexual humiliation inflicted by sexual violence against women, the next chapter furthers the case for risking feminist attachments to subjectivity. It also shows that such loosening of attachments does not undermine women's freedom, but rather promotes it by opening onto and fostering counter-normalizing modes of constituting, understanding, and relating to ourselves.

Notes

1 I am referring to Habermas's appeal to what he calls "transcendental-pragmatic presuppositions." These universal presuppositions are rules which are, Habermas argues, implicitly accepted by anyone who participates in practical discourse and which are in turn generated by or internal to that discourse itself; they are conditions for the possibility of rational argumentation as such (see Habermas 1999).

2 I understand by capacity a potentiality that may or may not be actualized. Nietzsche's view of capacities as effects of modes of self-understanding which are themselves effects of particular socio-historical contexts is consistent with the perspectives of Foucault and Butler as I present them.

3 Hatab (2005) refers specifically to Sections 17 and 19 of *Beyond Good and Evil* (Nietzsche 1989b, 24: 25–27). Nietzsche also refers to subjectivity as a linguistic phenomenon in the passage I cite from *On the Genealogy of Morals*, where he attributes its status as an ontological necessity to "the seduction of language" (1989a, 45).

4 See Foucault (1990a). From a Foucauldian perspective, then, men do not "have power" that women lack. Rather, persons normed as men (relative to persons normed as women) are able to more easily participate in or navigate relations of power and, hence, to shape the conditions of their own lives as well as societal structures and institutions.

5 Foucault writes:

> In effect, what defines a relationship of power is that it is a mode of action which does not act directly or immediately on others. Instead, it acts upon their actions: an action upon an action, in existing actions or on those which may arise in the present or in the future.
>
> (1983a, 220)

See also 1990a, where Foucault writes:

> . . . the rationality of power is characterized by tactics that are often quite explicit at the restricted level where they are inscribed . . . tactics which, becoming connected to one another, but finding their base of support and their conditions elsewhere, end by forming comprehensive systems.
>
> (95)

6 Foucault defines refusal, curiosity, and innovation as follows:

> refusal to accept as self-evident the things that are proposed to us; the need to analyze and to know, since we can accomplish nothing without reflection and knowledge – thus, the principle of curiosity; and the principle of innovation: to seek out in our reflection those things that have never been thought or imagined.
>
> (1980a)

7 Static power relations are not properly power at all, since power, insofar as it is relational, is by definition navigable and therefore at least to some extent dynamic. Static power is domination, a state rather than a set of relations; describing domination Foucault refers to "slavery" where humans are "in chains" (1983a, 221). While pure states of domination are probably rare, in my view, and relevant to the focus of this book, sexual slavery can be considered domination. Paradigmatic instances are those in which women are brought into the U.S. (or other countries) from abroad. The majority of such women do not speak the language of the country to which they are brought, their passports and other means by which they might endeavor to extricate themselves from the situation into which they are forced are confiscated, they are kept isolated, they are not told where (what state or city) they are being held, and they are sexually and physically brutalized on a daily basis. While rescue and especially escape from such a context is theoretically possible, the conditions for its possibility are deeply constrained (see Fernandez 2019).

8 I analyze how the concepts of the norm and normativity are implicated in normalizing relations of power in Taylor (2009).

9 Foucault's analysis of the ancient Greek self-relation focuses on Plato's Socratic dialogues; his analysis of the Greco-Roman self-relation draws upon Stoicism, Epicureanism, and Cynicism.

10 Foucault (2005). See especially the lectures of 13 January (first and second hours) and 20 January (first hour).

11 Foucault seems to consider the friendship of Seneca and Lucilius paradigmatic in this regard.

12 There is a "great image of turning around towards oneself underlying all the analyses I have been talking about," Foucault states (2005, 207).

13 Michel Snellart notes that in the 1980 course Foucault reconceptualizes the notion of regimes of truth in ways that reflect his specific concern with the process of subjectification. "Regime" in the 1980 course thus needs to be understood, Snellart explains, and as what I have presented makes clear, in terms of the "specific obligations an individual submits to in the act by which he becomes the agent of a manifestation of truth" (Snellart 2014, 341). Clearly reflected in

this notion of a regime of (and hence the conditions for the possibility of) truth, then, is the interconnection of enablement and constraint, self-assertion and self-renunciation.

14 This retention is apparent in the fact that individuals had to be prepared for the water ritual through the study of Christian teachings; they had to learn and believe in the truth of these teachings (2014, 105). "Acquisition of knowledge" prepared them for the "illumination" and purification that resulted from the water ritual (106).

15 Foucault explains that penitents are an "order" that exists between "catechumens," who are not yet Christians, and "fully practicing Christians" (2014, 196).

16 Michel Foucault, "Christianity and Confession." This is the second of the two Howison Lectures that Foucault delivered at UC Berkeley on October 20th and 21st of 1980. I am referencing the version that is housed in the IMEC Archives (Institut Mémoires de l'édition Contemporaine) (see Foucault 1980b). Slightly different versions of these lectures were delivered at Dartmouth College in November of 1980 (see Carrette 1999).

17 He analyzes these contexts in detail in his 1982 course, *The Hermeneutics of the Subject* (see Foucault 2005).

18 Foucault emphasizes that the work itself was significant rather than the actual attainment of perfection.

19 Foucault also states that this move in Descartes is solidified in Kant. This is apparent in the fact that for Kant, authority and by extension obedience become internally established in the form of autonomy: modern subjects subordinate themselves and are in turn rendered obedient to their own rational capacities. Constituting, understanding, and relating to oneself as a rational agent thus requires the continual renunciation of capacities deemed irrational or inconsistent with the dictates of reason. Elaboration of these points may be found in Foucault 1980c, 1997a, and 1997b.

2 Subjectivity, sexual violence, and sexual humiliation

When I began writing about sexual violence against women, I not surprisingly found myself repeatedly referring to it as harmful. This characterization seemed so obvious that for a time I didn't qualify what I meant by "harm." Upon setting out to provide clarification, I realized that, like many other feminist philosophers and theorists, I had been thinking about the harm of sexual violence in terms of objectification. I also realized that, for me, limiting the harm of sexual violence to objectification was no longer either appropriate or sufficient. Most obvious was the fact that the harm of being perceived and treated like an object depends upon the value of being seen and treated as a subject. Given my view of subjectivity as a normalizing mode of self-relation, I could no longer appeal to it in the name of conceptualizing and countering practices implicated in normalizing gendered relations of power. Additionally, though, it seemed to me that even if sexual violence did objectify women (which, given that subjectivity continues to function as the prevailing mode of self-relation, it seems safe to say that it does), that was not *all* that it did. Objectification, in other words, did not seem to me to be the sum total of the harm of sexual violence.

Reading about the Steubenville, Ohio, rape case was formative in my identifying humiliation as a fundamental harm of sexual violence against women. On the night of August 11, 2012, members of the Steubenville High School football team transported a sixteen-year-old girl who was incapacitated by alcohol (i.e., unconscious) between several end-of-summer parties (Macur and Schweber 2012). Postings the young men made to social media make multiple references to the rape of a "dead" girl; a photograph taken that night shows two of the men holding, respectively, the victim's arms and legs in order to move her about; in a cell-phone video one of the men engages in an extended, mocking commentary on the victim's assault (abcnews.go.com; Rol G 2013). Reflecting on this case, it seemed to me that humiliation was a fundamental element of the harm suffered by the victim; that all sexual violence, not only that committed by multiple perpetrators, humiliates; and, finally, that there was something distinctive about the specifically sexual humiliation inflicted by sexual violence.

Humiliation, I subsequently found, has generally been undertheorized within philosophy. Perhaps due to the existence of influential accounts provided by thinkers such as Sartre and Levinas, philosophers in the continental tradition tend to subsume humiliation under the auspices of shame. I address the distinction between shame and humiliation elsewhere (Taylor 2018b). Here, I aim to provide a full account of humiliation that elucidates the specific nature of sexual humiliation resulting from sexual violence. My account presents humiliation as a manifestation of the relation of self to self that both establishes itself by means of and intensifies definitive, normalizing features of subjectivity. As a redoubling of that intensification, sexual humiliation generates a deeply damaging relation of self to self. Ultimately, then, I implicate subjectivity in (re)producing not only a definitive harm of sexual violence and the conditions for its possibility, but also a mode of self-relation that is deficient in the capacities needed to counter both. The chapter thus illustrates the importance for feminism of loosening attachments to subjectivity. It also opens onto analysis in subsequent chapters of contemporary forms of feminist protest against sexual violence that reflect aspects of such loosening and thereby provide insight into alternative modes of self-relation.

I

Avishai Margalit provides a substantive account of humiliation in his book, *The Decent Society*. The book's title refers to Margalit's overarching argument that a decent society is one that does not humiliate its members. While he focuses on institutional conditions that humiliate, Margalit also addresses humiliation that occurs at the individual level. Whether the indirect effect of conditions of existence or a direct effect of behavior, humiliation is a distinctively human phenomenon. "There can be no humiliation," Margalit contends, "without human beings to bring it about" (1998, 10).[1]

Margalit presents humiliation as a violation of self-respect. To respect oneself, and to recognize others as possessing self-respect, is to see oneself and others as belonging to the human community (Margalit 1998). Self-respect for Margalit thus functions as a kind of base level of recognition; for him, to recognize another being as human provides "a ground for treating people equally" (44). What makes human beings worthy of respect is our capacity for freedom, which Margalit conceives in terms of self-transformation, or the potential to become in the future other than what one currently is. "All people are capable of living dramatically differently from the way they have lived so far," Margalit writes, and it is this capacity that "makes them human rather than mere things" (71; 119).

To violate self-respect and thereby humiliate proceeds by way of a double movement: seeing human beings as subhuman and subsequently treating them as if they are nonhuman. For Margalit, to see a being as human entails seeing the "body, especially the face and the eyes" as both capable of and in fact exhibiting particular modes of expression (1998, 94; 101).

He argues that when one observes the face and/or bodily comportment of another, one does not merely see lips that curve upward or downward, eyes that meet one's gaze or which are lowered, a head that is held high or "sunk down on the chest" (94). What we see, rather, is a characteristically human way of expressing a human way of experiencing a state or condition (happiness, sadness).[2] Subhuman entities, then, are seen as not (fully) experiencing and therefore (fully) expressing states and conditions in (fully) human ways. Margalit describes the corporeal expression of subhumanity in terms of "stigma," which may be either properly physical or conveyed on the body though, for example, forms of dress on the basis of which individuals are marked as inferior (103).[3] Consistent with Margalit's insights, Lisa Guenther argues that humiliation "singles out" and thereby individuates through a process of negation (2012, 61). Exposing or displaying individuals before either "real or imagined" others, it forces their visibility precisely "as no one or nothing" (Ibid).

Insofar as the capacity for freedom defines what it means to be human, subhuman entities will be seen as lacking in that capacity and therefore inhibited in their ability to become in the future anything other than subhuman. This lack both opens onto and is invoked in order to justify subhumans' unequal treatment, up to and including being treated "as if" they are nonhuman – treated, that is, in ways that completely deny individuals' capacity for freedom and duly reject them from the human community (Margalit 1998, 103; 112). Margalit's emphasis that humiliation entails treating humans *as if* they are rather than simply *as* nonhuman is important. Humiliation, he contends, requires recognition of the humanity of those it targets: "[t]he victim must be taken as someone with awareness, thus possessing implicit human worth, in order for an act of humiliation which denies his humanity to take place" (110). Like Margalit, Guenther contends that the radical singularity humiliation produces excludes individuals from humanity: it "severs relations between one person or group and a larger community" (2012, 61). At the same time, Guenther argues, this exclusion clarifies and strengthens the boundaries of and bonds within the community from which the humiliated individual has been expelled.

In sum, humiliating conditions and behaviors are those which see human beings as subhuman (possessing only a truncated capacity for freedom) and on the basis of that subhumanity treat them as if they were nonhuman (in ways that deny their capacity for freedom). Addressing the question of how the perspectives of and treatment by others can damage the respect one has for oneself and thereby produce the experience of humiliation, Margalit appeals to the interconnection of the self-relation with relations to others and world. "[T]he attitude of others," he writes,

> is required for determining what defines the commonwealth of mankind – a commonwealth that there is value in belonging to. The attitude of others is built into the very concept of the value of humans

which the bearer of self-respect is supposed to adopt with regard to herself . . . someone with self-respect is not exempt from taking into account the attitude of others toward her.

(1998, 124–125)

For Margalit, our experience of own value as human beings is derived from and reasserts the value of belonging within the broader human community. Insofar as the "identity traits" in and through which we constitute our relation to ourselves are simultaneously "belonging features," human beings cannot help but internalize and come to see ourselves in terms of external perspectives and treatment (133). Where humiliating conditions and treatment degrade identity traits, it is therefore not only the case that one is seen by others as subhuman; when one constitutes one's relation to oneself in terms of those traits, one becomes intelligible and recognizable to oneself – one comes to understand and relate to oneself – at least to some extent, in terms of one's own subhumanity. The interconnection of intelligibility and recognition with a radical curtailment of freedom undermines humiliated individuals' ability to transform their relationships to themselves. Put differently, the external curtailment or denial of freedom by others (i.e., the relationship to others and the world) becomes constitutive of the relation of self to self. This inhibiting of self-transformation helps to explain Margalit's description of the experience of being humiliated in terms of loss of control. "A considerable proportion of the most humiliating gestures," he writes, "are those which show the victims that they lack even the most miniscule degree of control over their fate – that they are helpless and subject to the good will (or rather, the bad will) of their tormentors" (116).

Margalit's and Guenther's work shows humiliation proceeding by way of, and in turn reproducing, defining characteristics of subjectivity. First, humiliation involves internalization. In a manner that reflects the interconnection of self-assertion with self-renunciation in the early Christian self-relation and the Cartesian subject (as discussed in Chapter 1), external perspectives of oneself as subhuman afford intelligibility at the same time that they make constitutive of the self-relation an aspect of itself that is deeply objectionable. That is, self-assertion (intelligibility and self-recognition) becomes interconnected with self-renunciation (subhumanity). Second, constituting, and thereby coming to understand and relate to oneself in terms of, subhumanity individuates. It singles one out by means of a negation that takes the form of exclusion from a community of beings in full possession of the capacity for freedom. Humiliation thus pushes the experience of oneself as a discrete and self-contained entity to its extreme limit of atomization and radical singularity.

Reproducing internalization and individuation in and of itself redoubles the normalizing character of subjectivity as a mode of self-relation. Normalization is further intensified by the fact that this internalization and individuation promote self-constitution, -understanding, and -relation in terms of debasement. In normalization generally, critical and creative capacities function in the service of constraint, which is experienced as enablement. Humiliation deploys enablement against itself. Turned back onto themselves as a source of degradation, critical and creative capacities, by means of which freedom is actualized, are potentially foreclosed.[4] This reconfiguration of the relationship between, and hence the very nature of, enablement and constraint intensifies the reflexive break Foucault describes grounding and by extension characterizing subjectivity as a mode of self-relation. Humiliation also compounds the self-renunciation and obedience that characterize subjectivity. Constituting, understanding, and relating to oneself in terms of exposure and display as subhuman, individuated and radically negated *before oneself*, not only curtails one's capacity for but also perverts one's relationship to one's own freedom, thereby fundamentally changing one's relationship to oneself.[5] Seeing itself as not only incapable but also *unworthy* of freedom, a humiliated self-relation is potentially unable to experience itself as other than subhuman. Experiencing oneself in this way opens onto treating oneself as if one were nonhuman – subjecting oneself to or submitting to being subjected to degradation. Humiliation ultimately threatens to fix the self-relation not merely in a cycle of asserting and renouncing itself, but in a permanent relation of abjection. Moreover, given the interconnection of self- and other/world relations, humiliation also compromises the capacity to resist and counter normalizing power relations more broadly. In short, then, humiliation has the potential to reduce a self-relation already compromised by normalization to a state of domination.[6]

II

The following working definitions, derived from the previous discussion, provide the basis for elucidating the nature of sexual humiliation experienced by victims/survivors of sexual violence.[7]

1   To humiliate is to see human beings as stigmatized in ways that render them subhuman and therefore lacking in the capacity for freedom, where freedom is construed in terms of self-transformation – becoming other than what one currently is. This view opens onto and legitimizes treating individuals as if nonhuman, in ways that deny their capacity for freedom and therefore reject them from the broader human community.
2   To be humiliated is to internalize external perceptions of oneself as subhuman and treatment of oneself as if one were nonhuman. Internalization entails being exposed and displayed before oneself as radically individuated: stigmatized, and therefore unworthy of freedom and inclusion in the human community.

First, then, it must be shown that sexual violence entails seeing women as stigmatized subhumans and treating them as if they were nonhuman.

Seeing women as subhuman

In his analysis of how it is possible for human beings to be seen as subhuman, Margalit observes that seeing is always informed and shaped by the normative conditions within which it occurs. "[W]hat we see," he writes, "is affected by what we habitually expect to see" (1998, 106). What we habitually expect to see, in turn, depends in large part on what is consistently available to be seen, on what registers as seeable. Prevailing ways of seeing become habitual through being socially legitimized, inculcated, and thus experienced simply as normal modes of perception.

Margalit's assertion that subhumanity is conferred as an effect of habitual seeing reflects key aspects of the normative cognitive process of framing posited by Judith Butler. As mentioned in Chapter 1, Butler argues that framing grants full recognition to some human lives but not to others. Consistent with the perspective that the self-relation is interconnected with relations to others and world,[8] Butler describes human existence as "precarious" – inherently social and therefore interconnected and interdependent (2010). The precarious nature of human existence means we have limited control over our actions and their effects: human beings cannot avoid either "impinging upon" or "being impinged upon by" our "exposure [to] and dependency [upon]" others (14). Precariousness is ambivalent in the sense that exposure to and dependence upon others is a source of both negative and positive experiences. "The very fact of being bound up with others," Butler contends, "establishes the possibility of being subjugated and exploited . . . [b]ut it also establishes the possibility of being relieved of suffering, of knowing justice and even love" (61).

By contrast, the unequal distribution of precariousness, which Butler refers to as precarity, is unequivocally harmful. Precarity takes the form of "politically," human-produced conditions under which some lives "suffer from failing social and economic networks of support" and are "*differentially* exposed" to harm in the forms of "injury, violence, and death" (Butler 2010, 25; my emphasis). It is framing, according to Butler, that generates precarity. The movement from intelligibility to recognition effectively casts some lives as not (fully) livable, thereby differentially exposing them to harm, at the same time that it (re)produces conditions under which precarity is construed as normal, uncritically accepted, and thus perpetuated. As Butler presents it, framing is "iterable," exclusionary, and normalizing. Iterability refers to the fact that frames "can only circulate by virtue of their reproducibility" (24). Through their continual reproduction, in other words, norms and normative processes become established as necessary aspects of existence – as reality as such. The conceptual narrowing that characterizes framing is exclusionary in the sense that anything which fails to fully register within a frame of recognition does not receive (full) ontological, epistemological, or moral consideration as a (fully) livable life. Moreover, just as Margalit presents subhumanity as being determined by habitual ways of seeing bodies – on the basis, that is, of stigmatization – Butler identifies embodiment as a key source and reflection of both precariousness and precarity. "That the body invariably comes up against the outside world," she writes, 'is a sign of the general predicament of unwilled proximity to others and circumstances beyond one's control . . . [t]his "coming up against" is one modality that defines the body' (34). While eliminating the body's "obtrusive alterity" would protect human beings from harms like sexual violence and sexual humiliation, it would also prevent us from experiencing pleasure, surprise, spontaneity, and hope. Given that precariousness is embodied, the differential exposure to negative impingement that may result from precarity will necessarily be embodied as well. "[I]t is this body, or these bodies, or bodies like this body or these bodies," Butler writes, "that live the condition of an imperiled livelihood, decimated infrastructure, accelerating precarity" (2015, 10).

Throughout her work, and as early as *Gender Trouble* (1990), Butler presents gender as a normalizing frame of recognition: gender distributes precariousness in ways that differentially expose women to precarity. Gendered relations of power function as a structure of recognizability characterized by two normative, mutually exclusive modes of recognition: (inferior) women and (dominant) men. Butler shows, moreover, that as an iterable process, gendered framing directs individuals' critical and creative capacities toward reproducing themselves as women and men to the point where gendered modes of self- and other relations become naturalized and therefore largely uncritically accepted; one might challenge gender oppression and seek to redefine gender norms while still viewing gender as necessary for making sense of self, other, and world. Consistent with normalization, gendered relations of power enable women (they afford intelligibility) by means of constraint (women gain recognition only as inferior beings). Inferiority thus both provides the basis for and characterizes the particular forms taken by women's stigmatization and subhumanity.

As Debra Bergoffen and Erinn Gilson illustrate, within the context of gendered power relations, simply being embodied as a woman is stigmatizing: women's sexed and sexualized bodies mark them as men's inferior others. Following Simone de Beauvoir, Bergoffen contends that women are not merely marked by but in fact "frozen" in their embodied sexualized otherness. Reducing women to "the sex" secures men's status as dominant subjects and in doing so insulates them from the exposure of embodiment and its interconnection with other/world relations (from, that is, the precariousness of existence) (Bergoffen 2017). "The hostility to the other and the assertion of absolute subjectivity," Bergoffen writes, "are reactionary flights from the inherent vulnerability of our intersubjective, ambiguous condition" (312). Gilson shows that women are marked in and reduced to the status of other on the basis not only of sexed but also sexualized embodiment. She identifies sexuality, itself social and embodied, as a key source of the exposure that characterizes *human* existence. Sexuality, Gilson argues, "initiates" humans as embodied beings "into a particular web of social significances in virtue of which we are especially open . . . to others" (2014, 150). Where men's dominant status is secured through disavowal of exposure resulting from sociality and embodiment, it makes sense that exposure resulting from sexuality will be attributed solely to women. This attribution is apparent in sexist constructions of women's sexualized embodiment. "If women are typically considered more vulnerable than men," Gilson argues,

> it is because of their bodies, which are deemed both weaker and more sexually stimulating . . . To be a woman is to inhabit the kind of body that is perceived as inciting lust and thus as inviting sexual attention, whether desired or not.
>
> $(152)^9$

Weakness, vulnerability in the sense of mere susceptibility to harm, and reductive sexualized embodiment lend themselves to a view of women as stigmatized beings that cannot (fully) experience and who are therefore incapable of expressing (fully) human states in (fully) human ways – to, in other words, a view of women as subhuman. Indeed, women are "recognized as human but inferior and [therefore] subordinated" (Bergoffen 2017, 313).

The truncated freedom that characterizes women's subhumanity takes a specific form. Bergoffen explains that women are permitted only the "illusion of freedom": they are "free" to reproduce their own inferiority, and to submit to that inferiority and the subordination it generates. If women were viewed and experienced themselves as possessing a (full) capacity for freedom and therefore self-transformation, their reproduction of themselves as subhuman could not be guaranteed, and gendered relations of power would be undermined. "Existing as loyal vassals," Bergoffen writes, "women use their freedom to become the mirror that confirms men in the illusion that they can escape the vulnerabilities and risks of their ambiguous humanity" (2017, 319). The perverted relationship to freedom that characterizes humiliation is thus already implicit in the gendered (self)perception of women as subhuman. Given that it is directed toward reproducing both the conditions for the possibility of their subhumanity and that subhumanity itself, women's freedom is effectively turned back on itself as a source of their inferiority and degradation. In short, women's stigmatization and subhumanity promote their (ideally, obedient) reproduction of their own subordination, as well as their conformity with the conditions for its possibility. Treating women as if they are nonhuman – in ways that deny their capacity for freedom – fully actualizes that relationship. While not all men see women as subhuman and not all those who do go on to treat women as if they are nonhuman, the normative framing of such seeing both facilitates and legitimizes treatment of women as if nonhuman by *particular* men by means of practices, like sexual violence, that (re)enforce and ultimately intensify women's subhumanity. To the extent that being treated as if nonhuman is taken as evidence of women's inherent inferiority, it appears to be justified. Such treatment therefore very effectively reproduces the gendered relations of power from which humiliating gendered practices emerge and gain their legitimacy.

Treating women as if they are nonhuman

Where women's freedom cannot be completely destroyed, with the result that their obedience cannot be unequivocally guaranteed, practices like sexual violence function to exact their continued reproduction of (or to at least reduce the possibility that they will undermine) gendered relations of power. Given that women's stigmatization and subhumanity are embodied and sexualized, sexual violence, which "targets the sexed body qua sexed," will be the most effective means by which to carry out this exacting or reducing (Bergoffen 2017, 313). Feminists have long recognized that by reining in individual women who might endeavor to direct their diminished freedom toward purposes other than reproducing and legitimizing men's dominance and their own inferiority and subhumanity, sexual violence simultaneously functions as a threat to all women. Writing in 1973, Karen Lindsey, Holly Newman, and Fran Taylor observe, "It is in the interest of the patriarchal system to condone rape while appearing to condemn it, for it is through rape that the anxieties which make women dependent on men physically, emotionally, morally, and legally, are reinforced" (2000, 195–196). Over forty years later, their observation is as relevant as ever: "Rape, the violence unleashed against women to humiliate them as the sex," Bergoffen asserts, "teaches them that their worth is tied to their status as the sex, and that the dignity of this status is determined by the lines drawn by men" (2017, 314).

Ann Cahill and Louise du Toit illustrate how rape, an embodied and sexualized violation, reinforces women's subhumanity and the conditions for its possibility by treating them as if they were nonhuman. Cahill defines rape as a "sexual, bodily attack on an embodied subject," the effect of which is to "undermine" in a "sexually specific" way an individual's "subjective integrity" (2001, 115). To refer to rape as *sexual* violence is thus to emphasize its use of "sexualized body parts and the very sexualities of the victim and assailant" in order to "commit physical, psychic, and emotional violence" (120). According to Cahill and du Toit, rape is possible because of both the embodied nature of the self-relation and its interconnection with the relations to others and the world – because, that is, of the embodied openness and exposure that characterize human existence in its precariousness. Because "self, world, and others constitute each other mutually," du Toit writes, they are "ontologically mutually dependent" (2009, 59). Akin to Butler, du Toit elaborates that in light of this interdependence, "we do not have privileged access to our selves or even our bodies and their meanings," nor are we the "architects" of our existence (Ibid).

Exploiting embodied openness and exposure, rape destroys the reciprocal character of the interconnection between self-relation and other/world relations: perpetrators exercise their capacities in order to deny victims the possibility of exercising theirs.[10] In rape, Cahill writes, "in a radical way, only one person (the assailant) is acting, and one person (the victim) is wholly acted on . . . stilled, silenced, overcome" (2001, 132). Arguing that rape victims are permitted merely to react – to respond only in ways that affirm the dominance of the assailant (e.g., through expressing fear or pleading not to be beaten or killed) – du Toit (2009) presents victims' immobilization precisely in terms of the turning of their capacity for freedom back onto itself. As mere reflections of the assailant's will, victims' "responses" are not properly responses at all; they are not expressions of the capacity for freedom but rather of its repression or absence. Given that rape effectively destroys the interconnection with others upon which self-constitution, -understanding, and -relation relies, Cahill argues that it ultimately constitutes a "bodily, sexual, assault on a woman's underlying conditions of being" (132). Profoundly undermining women's relationship to themselves, rape freezes victims in their sexualized, embodied, inferiority; in doing so, it denies their capacity to be anything other than subhuman – it denies, that is, their capacity for freedom. Like Bergoffen, both Cahill and du Toit describe this denial of women's freedom as bolstering a sense of dominance in the rapist, as well as the gendered relations of power that support men's domination more broadly. "In rape," du Toit writes, "masculine sexual identity as difference from and power over the feminine and female sexuality is what must be affirmed" (88). As Cahill puts it, "the rapist needs the destruction of the victim's being in order to construct his being as rapist" (133).

Cahill is clear that the embodied nature of sexual violence functions as a point of both intersection and difference in victims' experience of such violence. "Because all victims of rape are embodied," Cahill writes, "rape always has bodily significance" (2001, 115). Given the interconnection of self-relation and other/world relations, moreover, Cahill contends that despite the fact that no two individuals experience their embodiment in the same way, such experience is not merely singular. As I have emphasized, it is because "individual" experiences are shaped by external norms and relationships that they always extend beyond the self-relation, that they are at the same time social and thus in important ways shared. Embodiment, Cahill argues, is thus neither "radically" individual nor individuating (114). Put in Butler's terms, while no two experiences of (or responses to) the precariousness of human existence are the same, human beings do share the experience of "coming up against" other human beings precisely as bodies. At the same time, Cahill emphasizes that "because embodiment is marked by difference, [bodily] significance varies widely among victims" (115). She describes, for example, how systemic racism in the U.S. shapes the meaning of rape generally as well as interracial rape more specifically in ways that affect how victims (and perpetrators) experience it. Cahill further notes that factors, including but not limited to age, physical ability, sexual orientation, and socioeconomic status, contribute to both the experience of embodiment and its violation through sexual violence. Like du Toit, Namrata Mitra (2018) shows how the legacy of colonization produces a variety of modes of feminine embodiment that result in vastly different meanings and experiences of sexual violence among particular groups within postcolonial societies. Bergoffen (2011) provides a similar analysis of modes of embodiment within contexts where rape is deployed as a weapon of war.

The specifically gendered and sexualized manifestations of stigmatization, subhumanity, and treatment as if nonhuman that occur in sexual violence are reflected in women's experience of sexual humiliation. Implicit in Cahill's description of rape as an assault on the conditions of victims' being (in my terms, on their attachment to themselves) is the internalization by victims of these external perceptions and treatment and, hence, the experience of sexual humiliation by victims. Du Toit explicitly argues that "[v]ictims of rape tend to internalize the view of themselves as projected by the rapist" (2009, 85). Consistent with what I have presented in this chapter, she describes this external view in terms of stigmatization: "victims are reduced to [their] bodies" and therefore to the "pain and humiliation" to which they, as embodied beings, have been subjected (Ibid). This internalization of being reduced to the harm they have experienced (their own pain and humiliation) individuates victims. While rape exposes sexualized aspects of both victims' and perpetrators' bodies, du Toit observes that assailants' nakedness is overshadowed for victims by horror at and subsequent preoccupation with their own (2009, 83). This horror and preoccupation stem from the fact that rape confronts victims with and produces an experience of themselves – it displays them before themselves – in terms of the violation that stigmatization and subhumanity entail. The internalization of the denial of freedom that occurs during rape, in other words, takes the specific form of experiencing oneself (merely) in terms of one's own violation.

It is not difficult to see how the experience of sexual humiliation produced by sexual violence intensifies the interconnection of self-assertion with self-renunciation that characterizes subjectivity as a mode of self-relation. Being reduced to a violation of oneself, as du Toit puts it, binds self-recognition to "self-aversion" (2009, 85). In my view, the self-blame which, as du Toit notes, sexual violence often invokes in victims reflects their constitution and understanding of, and relation to, themselves in terms of the denial of their freedom that occurred while they were being raped. Put differently, self-blame expresses the truncated freedom of subhumanity that is unique to victims. It expresses a particularly objectionable channeling of critical and creative capacities toward the reproduction of one's own subhumanity in which victims see themselves as unworthy of and thus deny their own capacity for freedom by implicating themselves in their violations (84). Victims blame themselves, du Toit argues, because they survived; only their death would indicate that they had done everything possible to prevent being attacked. Surviving "leaves the rape victim feeling as if she had made a pact with the devil, had sold some part or aspect of herself in order to retain something of herself" (85). Self-blame resulting from sexual violence reflects a mode of self-relation in which one experiences one's own existence, the very fact of being alive, as a renunciation of oneself. In its most extreme manifestations, self-assertion is possible only through death, the ultimate negation.

III

The examples I consider in this section of the chapter illustrate just three of the myriad ways in which sexual violence humiliates, as well as the nature of women's experience of sexual humiliation. In her book, *Femininity and Domination*, Sandra Bartky describes the following scenario:

> It is a fine spring day, and with an utter lack of self-consciousness, I am bouncing down the street. Suddenly I hear men's voices. Catcalls and whistles fill the air. These noises are clearly sexual in intent and they are meant for me; they come from across the street. I freeze.
>
> (1990, 27)[11]

Bartky's description of herself as freezing reflects the experience Bergoffen describes of women being frozen as "the sex." Being stopped in her tracks by these men's voices reflects Bartky's internalization of her stigmatization and, therefore, her subhumanity. It is on the basis of her body – her "bouncing breasts" of which she was not even aware until that moment – that she is singled out and fixed in her stigmatization. She is, as she writes, reduced merely to a "'nice piece of ass'" (Ibid). This fixing and reduction, as well as her own freezing in response to them, likewise reflect the fact that she has been treated in a way that denies her capacity to be anything else. Significantly, Bartky describes the internalization of these men's perspectives; she has not only been subjected to humiliating perspectives and treatment, she has experienced humiliation. These men, she asserts, could simply have watched her pass by and stayed silent. But they have rather forced her awareness of the fact that she has been reduced to her own embodied stigma. She has been displayed before herself as subhuman. "I must," Bartky writes, "be made to see myself as they see me" (Ibid).

My second example concerns thirteen women who were raped and sexually assaulted by Daniel Holtzclaw during his tenure as an Oklahoma City police officer. All of Holtzclaw's victims were Black women; all but one resided in economically disenfranchised neighborhoods. Holtzclaw stopped women on the street, detained them, and then checked to see if they had outstanding arrest warrants or were perhaps under the influence of alcohol or drugs (Testa 2015). In cases where a woman's circumstances were in fact compromised, Holtzclaw threatened her with incarceration in order to inhibit resistance when he subsequently sexually assaulted and/or raped her. He harassed some victims on multiple occasions, coming to their homes, calling them on the telephone, and sending them text messages. Holtzclaw stopped Jannie Ligons one night on the premise that she was driving erratically. Despite the fact that Ligons was in fact not a resident of but simply passing through the neighborhood Holtzclaw targeted and had no incriminating circumstances that he could wield against her, he still detained and sexually assaulted her (Fenwick and Schwarz 2015; Lindsey 2015; Testa 2015).

That Holtzclaw's victims are viewed as subhuman (by him as well as more broadly) is apparent in the particular nature of the precarity of their conditions of existence, conditions which simultaneously disproportionately expose them to and inhibit recognition of harm. This sexual exposure can be seen as an aspect of but is not reducible to the sexualization of women's bodies that leaves them perpetually open to "sexual attention." It also reflects Black women's historical status as mere property under slavery, as well as racist depictions of them as hypersexual, both of which cast them as "unrapeable." Indeed, rape laws in some U.S. states originally excluded Black women (Davis 1998; West and Johnson 2016). As Angela Davis argues, this historical legacy continues to shape racist views of Black women as always sexually available, especially to white men; sexualized, racist depictions of women of color in popular media provide ample evidence of this point (1998). That these racist views have actual material effects on women's lives is apparent in the fact that Black women not only report higher rates of sexual objectification than white women (as well as accompanying heightened levels of concern for their physical safety and psychological distress) but that they actually experience higher rates of sexual violence (West and Johnson 2016; Planty et al. 2016). At the same time that Black women are disproportionately exposed to sexual violence, however, they report it to the police at lower rates than white women. This under-reporting makes sense given, as Davis notes, the oppression communities of color continue to experience at the hands of the police, oppression that includes rape of women by male police officers (1998). Consistent with Davis's analysis, none of Holtzclaw's first twelve victims reported his crimes to law enforcement. That only Ligons did so illustrates how socioeconomic disenfranchisement (itself a legacy of slavery) intersects with race and gender in ways that magnify the precarity of poor Black women.

The relative lack of media attention generated by the Holtzclaw case illustrates how the precarity of the victims' lives exacerbates and is in turn exacerbated by the view of them as subhuman (Ford 2015).[12] Until the rendering of the verdict, the *New York Times*, which provided extensive coverage of the Steubenville case, relied upon stories from other media outlets such as the Associated Press. Most worthy of attention for many mainstream news sources seemed to be the question of whether the all-white jury would find Holtzclaw guilty.[13] As I note elsewhere, sexual violence against women generally is met with ambivalence (Taylor 2018a). This ambivalence reflects the normative view of women as subhuman; sexual violence against fully livable lives would be definitively denounced. At the same time, and despite the fact that Holtzclaw was ultimately convicted and sent to prison, the lack of outrage on behalf of his "imperfect" victims illustrates the extent to which framing casts the subhumanity of (especially poor) women of color in ways that make them and the harms committed against them more difficult to recognize (McLaughlin, Sidner, and Martinez 2016).[14] This lack of outrage reflects a form of victim-blaming in which conditions of intensified precarity are considered normal for women of color *because of who they are*. As Charles Mills puts it, "the norming of the individual is partially achieved by spacing it . . . representing it as imprinted with the characteristics of a certain kind of space" (1997, 42). Such "norming and racing of space" effectively blames poor women of color for what happens to them within the context of those conditions (41).

Holtzclaw's serial sexual predation, the nature of his crimes, and the fact that he sought out women whose disproportionate disempowerment deeply compromised their ability to resist illustrate the extent to which he treated these women as if they were nonhuman. His actions illustrate a particularly egregious manner of fixing women in their embodied, sexualized subhumanity and thereby denying their capacity to be anything other than subjugated. Holtzclaw not only raped and sexually assaulted women, he presented these violations as benefitting them – a courtesy to keep them out of jail. Framing the situation in this manner – a "choice" between sexual violation and incarceration – Holtzclaw effectively implicates the women in and thus, as noted above, blames them for their own assaults: he is merely doing what the women have "chosen" for him to do. "It's better than county [lockup]," he told one of his victims before assaulting her (Testa 2015). Holtzclaw's humiliation of victims is also apparent in his targeting of women who were unable to resist not only during the assault but whom, he believed, due to their compromised circumstances could never resist, could never report what he had done to them. That, until Jannie Ligons, victims did not in fact report, as well as their reasons for not doing so, can be seen as evidence that they experienced humiliation. The view that one will not be believed, that harms committed against one will not be recognized as harms, may reflect internalization of a broader view of oneself as subhuman and the effects of subsequently being treated as if nonhuman. "I didn't call [the police]," related one victim. "To be honest, I don't like the police and I try to stay away from them as far as I can" (Ibid). A second victim explained, "Who are they going to believe? It's my word against his because I'm a woman and . . . he's a police officer. So I just left it alone and just prayed that I never saw this man again" (Ibid). Consistent with these perspectives, a third woman relates, "I spoke only in passing about it maybe once or twice, but I never went into details about it with anybody. I didn't – I just try not to think about it" (Ibid). I think these women's remarks graphically express Bartky's contention that being sexually humiliated is "like being made to apologize" (1990, 27). Insofar as sexual humiliation, like sexual violence, reinforces women's inferiority and subjugation, blaming them – making them apologize – for what they have endured effectively twists the knife of the initial sexual violation.

My third example encompasses the Steubenville case, which I described at the outset of this chapter, and a similar Canadian case. Rehtaeh Parsons, a fifteen-year-old girl from Halifax, Nova Scotia, was impaired by alcohol when she was assaulted. A photograph taken by another young man who was present at the time shows Parsons vomiting out a window while being penetrated from behind by her assailant, who is giving a thumbs-up signal (Gillis 2013). Cressida Heyes argues in an analysis of rape and sexual assault of semiconscious or unconscious victims that the "capacity for anonymity" is not distinct from but in fact part of lived experience (2016). Insofar as this is the case, the anonymity afforded by a retreat from consciousness is constitutive of, not distinct from or opposed to, the relation of self to self; being able to withdraw from the world defines the self-relation as much as the ability to reach out into it. This ability to withdraw, Heyes argues, is especially important for people whose lives are characterized by the kind of exposure and visibility I have described as accompanying precarity. Heyes focuses on the state of unconsciousness obtained in sleep, which, she asserts, "brings a special kind of respite" for oppressed persons (372). Sexual assault and rape committed against the semi- and unconscious are therefore especially egregious: these acts violate a fundamental dimension of self-constitution in which individuals are arguably at their most vulnerable. This violation, according to Heyes, is "extended . . . when a community of voyeurs is created around" images that are taken and distributed of these victims (Ibid).

Heyes's analysis provides important insight into the humiliating perspectives and treatment to which the Steubenville victim and Rehtaeh Parsons were subjected. The two victims can be seen to have been reduced to merely sexualized bodies available for the use of others. These young women's respective unconscious and semi-conscious states, as well as the fact that their violations were documented in images, reflect their reduction to subhumanity and, therefore, denial of their freedom. Sexually violating someone who is unaware or only vaguely aware of what is happening accomplishes the aim of generating only *re*actions desired by the perpetrator in a different way than sexual violence committed against conscious individuals. What the perpetrator wants at the time of the assault in these cases is not to generate a particular reaction that reflects the victim's helplessness, indicates that she is experiencing lack of control, and thereby affirms the perpetrator's sense of dominance. Incapacitated and impaired victims manifest that helplessness in their entire mode of embodiment. Incapacitated victims are not only motionless; they lack the capacity for any sort of response other than merely physical ones that reflect lack of control (vomiting, as in the Parsons case, as well as, for example, urinating on oneself). Impaired victims may be able to move, but their movements also reflect a lack of control – slurred or incoherent speech, swaying, falling down, or being unable to stand at all. These kinds of corporeal expressions of helplessness may be taken to heighten victims' stigmatization and, therefore, their subhumanity.

Exploiting and especially reveling in corporeal manifestations of helplessness treats victims as if they are not human in ways that intensify their humiliation. This same dynamic is apparent in the Holtzclaw case, with race, gender, socioeconomic status, and geographical location serving as stigmatized corporeal manifestations not necessarily of helplessness (although, as I note, some of Holtzclaw's victims were impaired when he assaulted them) but of social marginalization that compromised their capacity for resistance and facilitated Holtzclaw's affirmation of his dominant status as both a man and a police officer. Moreover, just as Holtzclaw intentionally targeted victims whose lives were characterized by intensified precarity, so do men intentionally target impaired and incapacitated women. A recent study found that ninety percent of "sexually aggressive incidents" in bars involved men's actions toward women. The men's "level of invasiveness was related to intoxication of the targets, but not their own intoxication, suggesting intoxicated women were being targeted" (Graham et al. 2014).

When I presented an early version of this work at my departmental colloquium, a colleague questioned whether incapacitated or impaired victims could experience humiliation since they would not have been aware of being violated and would have no or incomplete memory of it. As Heyes notes, images of incapacitated and impaired victims extend their violation (2016). Images also provide the possibility for such victims to experience humiliation after the fact. These images confront victims with how they have been viewed and treated; they are displayed before themselves in their view as subhuman and treatment as if they were nonhuman. The images, in short, provide the experience Bartky describes as "being-made-to-be-aware of one's own flesh" (1990, 27). Her testimony at the trial of assailants Trent Mays and Ma'lik Richmond indicates that the Steubenville victim had only scant memory of the night of her assault and no memory of the assault itself. She stated that when she regained consciousness she was "under a blanket in an unfamiliar place surrounded by three boys;" she was "embarrassed, scared, not sure what to think" (Simpson 2013). Second-hand accounts (from friends who were angry at the victim and blamed her for her assault), but primarily the images that were posted to social media and circulated within the community informed the victim about what had happened to her. The community of voyeurs created by the sharing of such images functions, as noted by Guenther (2012), to underscore for victims their singularity and thus the fact of their rejection from the human community. Both the Steubenville victim and Rehtaeh Parsons returned to school to find groups of students huddled around cell phones viewing images of them being sexually violated, the images were sent from phone to phone, and also posted to the Internet for even broader consumption. Both young women were subsequently socially ostracized: friends turned against them; Parsons changed school multiple times.

The victim-blaming that occurred in the Steubenville and Parsons cases illustrates a different way in which the experience of sexual humiliation is like being made to apologize. While any victim of sexual violence may experience it, self-blame has been shown to be heightened for impaired victims and at its most extreme for those who were incapacitated when they were assaulted (Grubb and Turner 2012).[15] This intensification stems in part from the fact that intoxication violates norms of femininity, such that women who are sexually violated while under the influence of alcohol (as well as other substances) are often considered to be receiving deserved punishment. "Victims of rape who are intoxicated are held more responsible and more to blame for the rape" than non-intoxicated victims;[16] conversely, intoxicated perpetrators, are viewed as "less responsible for their actions than sober perpetrators" (2012, 448). The Steubenville victim and Rehtaeh Parsons were doubly blamed and would thus doubly blame themselves for becoming intoxicated and ostensibly facilitating their assaults, as well as for the assaults themselves. Having only partial or no memory of one's assault would also exacerbate the self-blame of humiliation. Just as one blames oneself for consuming alcohol, one blames oneself for not being able to recall what happened to oneself, as well as for having to rely on external sources for that information. Moreover, second-hand accounts, partial memory, and the images with which impaired and incapacitated victims may be confronted raise a whole host of questions which, insofar as they cannot be answered, may haunt victims/survivors in ways that further exacerbate their humiliation and the interconnection of self-recognition with the self-aversion it inculcates. Can the accounts of others be trusted? Is my memory accurate? What did they do to me that I do not remember? The anguish victims experience after being assaulted illustrates Margalit's point that humiliation is experienced as an existential threat (Margalit 1998, 122).

Just as Cahill sees rape functioning as an assault on women's mode of being, then, I see the humiliation of sexual violence acting as an assault on women's relationship to – their attachment to – themselves. By making it simultaneously essential and repugnant, sexual humiliation tears at the fabric of that attachment. This, then, is the specific character of the cycle of self-assertion and -negation in which sexual humiliation mires the relation of self to self. Parsons's suicide can be seen as evidence of this point, particularly as it reflects the intensification of self-blame experienced by impaired and incapacitated victims. Her act reflects the ultimate apology insofar as it suggests that she considered herself as not only unworthy of freedom but of life itself.[17]

IV

Before concluding, I want to address the question of whether all victims of sexual violence will experience humiliation. Margalit's treatment of this issue relative to humiliation in general is a bit complicated. According to my argument that the self-relation is formed in and through broader norms as well as relations to others and world, individuals cannot help but internalize to at least some extent norms and external perspectives. At the same time, and consistent with Margalit, I want to suggest that human beings are able to deploy defensive techniques which, while they may "mitigate" its effects, ultimately neither prevent nor eradicate humiliation. In support of this perspective, Margalit describes a variety of tactics Jews have employed in deflecting humiliating persecution. Viewing Nazis as monsters and therefore *inhuman*, he asserts, protected Jews against being confronted with their exclusion from the *human* community. Viewing persecuting gentiles in general as "barking dogs" or turning them into figures of fun serves a similar purpose since barking dogs may be frightening but they cannot humiliate, and ridiculous people are not to be taken seriously at all (Margalit 1998, 122–123). At the same time, Margalit argues that because the persecutors *are* in fact human, "the [experience of] humiliation exists, and it is justified" (122). Moreover, given the self-relation's interconnection with others and world, despite our best efforts at disavowal, the perspectives of others are ultimately constitutive of our relationship to ourselves. Indeed, if this were not the case, deflecting humiliation through defensive techniques would not be necessary. So, even if defensive techniques worked, Margalit contends, "the humiliating situation would remain" (122). What I see him saying here is that humiliating conditions and behaviors are humiliating in their own right, because they entail perceiving as subhuman and treating as if nonhuman. The fact that evidence of the experience of humiliation on the part of targeted individuals does not determine humiliation's conditions of possibility is important; it means that societies that produce humiliating conditions and individuals who engage in humiliating behavior are culpable even without such evidence. Whether or not they were aware or fully aware of it at the time, the Steubenville victim and Rehtaeh Parsons were viewed as subhuman and treated as if they were nonhuman; these young women were subjected to humiliation when they were assaulted.

Nicola Gavey's work sheds light on how women who are cognizant of humiliating conditions and treatment to which they are subjected may deploy defensive mechanisms against both. Focusing on what she refers to as the "cultural scaffolding of rape" – normative gender roles and norms of heterosex that comprise conditions for the possibility of rape and its broad uncritical acceptance – Gavey shows that a whole spectrum of ethically problematic sexual encounters exists between sex that is desired by the parties involved and sexual assault and rape (Gavey 2005). This indeterminate "gray area" of "unsexy," "unwanted," and "coercive" sex emerges from the intersection of traditional yet still prevalent norms of gender, heterosexuality, and heterosex. Particularly prominent, from Gavey's perspective, are norms surrounding men's sexual aggression and women's sexual passivity, and the "coital imperative" which reduces heterosex to intercourse; heterosex thus becomes defined in terms of men's sexuality generally and their sex drive more specifically (2005, 225). Where men are constructed as not only wanting but indeed requiring sex, their pressuring of women to engage in intercourse is seen as normal. Constructed as needing to be made to want intercourse, by contrast, women are de facto in the position of having to decide whether or not to "give" or "allow" it.[18] By casting them simply as normal heterosexual interactions, normative gender and heterosex legitimize and therefore encourage the kinds of situations that characterize the sexual gray area.

While a "rational autonomous actor" might be able to unambiguously draw the line between what it does and does not want and therefore definitively refuse the latter, Gavey shows that normative gender and heterosex make it difficult for women to refuse men's sexual advances. Under these norms "it would not be right or fair for a woman to stop sex before male orgasm" (Gavey 2005, 121).[19] Hence, Gavey's point that when she speaks of "unwanted sex," she does not mean simply that women may on occasion engage in intercourse with men when they do not really feel like it, but rather that women's experience of their own sexuality is characterized by an experience of being obligated to do so. Interviews Gavey conducted with women about their sexual experiences reveal the "absence of a language for saying no" and the subsequent inability on the part of women "to actually say it" (144). Gavey further points out that blunt refusal violates norms governing communication generally, and especially, as noted above, norms of femininity.[20]

Gavey's illustration of the extent to which "[d]irectly refusing unwanted sex potentially compromises the performance of femininity in ways that a woman may find extremely difficult to embody" offers important insight into the relations of power that make it easier for women to say yes than to say no, even when the sex is unwanted, unpleasant, or coercive (2005, 145). While I will analyze the broader #MeToo phenomenon in the next chapter, it is worth noting here how Gavey's work helps to make sense of the actions of "Grace," the woman who accused actor Aziz Ansari of sexual assault, as well as Ansari's own behavior (Way 2018).[21] Masculine sex drive discourse, the coital imperative, as well as broader constructions of normative gender and heterosex can be seen to have shaped that encounter in significant ways – from Ansari's persistence to the fact that Grace engaged in sexual activity with which she was not comfortable and remained in his apartment after the unwanted sex occurred. Gavey also, then, provides a welcome counter-perspective to those which, in positing Grace as the unfettered autonomous agent, contend that she could and therefore should have simply and easily extricated herself from Ansari and left his apartment. Gavey's work elucidates the complexities of gender as an effect of a normalizing relations of power that is, as I have mentioned, in many ways compelling for women even as they are oppressed by it. No woman is free from the constraints of femininity; all are therefore constrained, albeit to greater and lesser degrees and in myriad different ways, by the negative external perception of women who refuse sex to men. Women whose self-relation is shaped in large part by normative gender and heterosex are "less likely" than others "to have an alternative framework from which to more positively interpret [their] actions" (Gavey 2005, 156).

The (hetero)sexual gray area Gavey describes both reflects and reasserts the view of women as subhuman generated within gendered relations of power more broadly. It illuminates, for example, the contradiction of casting women as "rational" and "autonomous" beings who are accountable for policing their own sexual activity, and gendered and heterosexual norms that constrain their ability to do so. Specifically, the convergence of gender and heterosex, as reflected in masculine sex-drive discourse and the coital imperative, leave women with at least inadequate capacities for identifying unwanted and coercive sexual practices; for articulating why those practices are unwanted and coercive; and, therefore, for refusing to engage in those practices. A diminished capacity for being able to refuse what is not wanted facilitates a view of women as possessing less than a full capacity for freedom, a view that, as I have shown, opens directly onto treatment that completely denies that capacity.

Indeed, Gavey's interviewees describe multiple instances in which men treated them as if they were nonhuman by overtly denying their "ability to shape" the trajectory of a sexual encounter (2005, 121). One woman describes a "terrifying" encounter with a man who violently forced himself on her (he bit her and also left her bruised) (159). From Gavey's perspective, this woman was "subjected to intercourse against her will – and it could be argued that this was forced or, at least, carried out through threat of force or implied threat of force" (160). At the same time, the woman does not consider herself to have been raped because, she explains to Gavey, she "'acquiesced''' *before rape could occur*; as Gavey puts it, she "strategically" went along with "forced sex" (Ibid). This woman's situation meets my definition of a humiliating situation. That she is viewed as subhuman (possessing as best a diminished capacity to determine whether or not she wants to engage in sexual intercourse) is apparent in the man's lack of consideration for her capacity for refusal; moreover, she is treated in a manner that denies her capacity to be anything other than sexually available to him. In my view, her framing of the encounter as reluctant consensual sex rather than rape reflects the sort of attempt to deflect humiliation Margalit describes. Seeing herself as having gone along with or at least not refused sex allows this woman to retain a sense of control that mediates against her seeing herself as a being who has been viewed as subhuman and treated as if she were unworthy of becoming anything else. It allows her, in other words, to deflect the total loss of control that rape, as described by Cahill and du Toit, involves. For this woman, Gavey writes,

> the critical element to be avoided was the potential to be in a situation where it was *unambiguously clear* that she had *absolutely no* control. If she could retain enough control to avoid getting to that point . . . then it was somehow probably preferable.
>
> (160; original emphasis)

In contrast to the Jewish tactic of dehumanizing persecutors as a way of mitigating humiliation, in minimizing the severity of her experience, this woman, like others Gavey interviewed, seems to be *humanizing* the man who harmed her. If he is not a rapist, then she has not been raped. This tactic makes sense in the cases of the women who were in relationships with the men who abused them; it's possible something more like the dehumanization Margalit describes is operative in cases of stranger rape.

Gavey dedicates an entire chapter of her book to addressing the fraught question of how to categorize instances in which women whose experience of forced sex meets a legal or other definition of rape but who do not consider themselves to have been raped. Another interviewee described to Gavey an occasion upon which she awoke to find her male roommate in her bed "groping" her (2005, 161). Similar to the account provided above, this woman did not try to stop the man when he proceeded to have intercourse with her because she thought that if she resisted he would rape her (161). At the same time, this woman expressed to Gavey that "'he did anyway, sort of thing, really, when you think about it, when I look back'" (161). While she acknowledges that by many accounts this woman's experience can be conceptualized as rape, as well as that the woman herself seems to identify it as rape during the interview, Gavey nonetheless relates that "from the point of view of a feminist research ethic, I would struggle with the validity and ethics of labeling [this woman] as a rape victim at the time when she did not choose this label herself" (178). Gavey is very clear that she is not casting her interviewees as engaging in some sort of false consciousness. Her aim, rather, is to once again draw attention to the extent to which normative gender and heterosex inhibit women's ability to make sense of their own experience and, in doing so, compromise their ability to resist and counter harms committed against them. This ambiguity, Gavey argues, "invites cultural critique of the realm of heterosexual possibility that can contain such offensive, disrespectful and . . . hurtful male acts" (178).

V

Like Gavey, I am not arguing that women who deploy defensive techniques against what I would define as sexually humiliating perspectives and treatment are engaging in false consciousness. The target of my criticism is not women's responses to humiliating conditions and treatment but the conditions and treatment themselves, as well as the gendered relations of power within which sexual humiliation not only emerges, but gains legitimacy and broad uncritical acceptance. Given the potential of humiliation to inflict severe damage to the self-relation, deploying defensive tactics against it makes perfect sense. At the same time, I agree with Margalit that such tactics are ultimately ineffective; by simply deflecting humiliation, they leave in place the conditions for its possibility. Defensive mechanisms reflect and in turn reassert a merely reactive element within the relation of self to self. In the case of women who have experienced sexual violence, sexual humiliation becomes constitutive, even as it is masked over by asserting positive self-images such as "survivor" or less negative self-images such as "reluctant consenter but not rape victim." Insofar as the same norms enable and constrain the relation of self to self, self-transformation cannot be as simple as rejecting "bad" norms or substituting "good" or less bad norms for them. A reactive self-image and the self-relation constituted in terms of it remain bound up with the experience of, and as a response to, the humiliation in which they are forged. Deflection leaves unchallenged, and implicitly reasserts through creating the need for its continual renunciation, the external perspective of the self-relation as subhuman.

My analysis shows that appealing to subjectivity in order to counter sexual humiliation needs to be seen as a kind of defensive and therefore ultimately ineffective technique. Constituting, understanding, and relating to oneself as a subject entails constituting, understanding, and relating to oneself in terms of the individuation and internalization that enable and characterize humiliation. Invoking subjectivity in order to counter the harm of sexual violence masks this interconnection and thereby reasserts its violation; when that harm in turn becomes constitutive of who one is, one attaches to oneself in terms of it. While this chapter has detailed the depth and complexity of women's constraint in their ability to constitute, understand, and relate to themselves differently, it is important to recall that normalization generally and the normalizing self-relation promoted by sexual humiliation more specifically may *but need not* destroy women's capacity for freedom. Butler writes that the simultaneity of enablement and constraint that characterizes normalizing norms presents an opportunity to discern in our conformity "the sign of [our] constraint" (Butler 2004, 191). She also identifies possibilities for "resistance" or "opposition" in the moment "when we find ourselves attached to our constraint, and so constrained in our very attachment" (191–192). Part of what I take from these important insights is that we can identify ways in which our attachments to ourselves are formed in and through and therefore reproduce our aversion to ourselves, and that such identification opens onto possibilities for the loosening of such attachments that is self-transformation. As I state in Chapter 1, once we see that normalization is not domination, normalization's ubiquity can open onto multiple sites for its countering. Returning to

Foucault's work, the next two chapters analyze specific forms of feminist protest that possess counter-normalizing potential relative to sexual violence and sexual humiliation.

Notes

1 In contrast to my conceptualization of it, Margalit conceives of humiliation as a feeling.
2 It's not clear to me whether Margalit is saying that only humans can express certain states or conditions. It does seem clear, however, that he is saying that there are distinctively human ways of expressing states and conditions.
3 Margalit cites the "beards and sidecurls" of "ultra-Orthodox Jews" and "the galabiya, turban, and Assyrian beard of Islamic fundamentalists" as examples of stigmatizing dress (1998, 103).
4 The dynamics by means of which humiliation produces a break within the self-relation strongly resemble those by means of which, as Elaine Scarry describes it, torture accomplishes the same thing. Torture simultaneously truncates, internalizes, and redeploys in the service of self- and world-destruction the embodied capacities through which we experience our relationship to ourselves, and by means of which we extend ourselves into and therefore experience the world – by means of which, in other words, we expand our experience. "Each source of strength and delight, each means of moving out into the world or moving the world in to oneself," Scarry writes, "becomes a means of turning the body back onto itself, forcing the body to feed on the body" (Scarry 1985, 48).
5 Again, what I'm describing here is analogous to the way in which torture perverts individuals' experience of their own embodiment (see Scarry 1985).
6 According to Margalit, some concentration camp survivors report that they found the severe humiliation they experienced in the camps more damaging than the physical cruelty. While he also acknowledges that individuals for whom this was the case are not representative of all Holocaust survivors, given the horror of the camps these perspectives are instructive concerning the level of harm humiliation is capable of inflicting (see Margalit 1998, 136).
7 Although Margalit's appeal to self-respect, equality, and humanity may appear to invoke a sort of Kantianism that conflicts with my Foucauldian perspective, his grounding of these notions in a conceptualization of freedom construed as the capacity for self-transformation resonates strongly with Foucault's work. If to be treated as equal is to be treated as a being with the capacity to become other than what one currently is, I don't think Margalit's notion of equality conflicts with Foucault's contention that power relations are never equal; Margalit can be seen, rather, to be invoking the notion that human beings have the capacity to navigate power relations.
8 "One finds," Butler writes,

> that the only way to know oneself is through a mediation that takes place outside of oneself, exterior to oneself, by virtue of a convention or norm one did not make, in which one cannot discern oneself as an author or agent of one's own making.
>
> (2005, 28)

9 Gilson notes that this construction of feminine embodiment effectively "naturalizes [sexual] violence (as an inevitable outcome of male aggression and female violability)" (2014, 152).
10 "In rape," du Toit writes, "sexual differentiation takes the form of desubjectifying womanhood so that manhood or the masculine may appear by contrast

as the subject par excellence, pure abstraction and pure will independent of physical and accidental existence" (2009, 83).

11 I am grateful to Erinn Gilson for drawing my attention to how effectively Bartky's description illustrates humiliation as I conceive of it.

12 Matt Ford notes the scant coverage in *The Atlantic* (see Ford 2015). The Huffington Post provided comprehensive coverage of the case: www.huffington post.com/news/daniel-holtzclaw/.

13 Holtzclaw's father is white and his mother is Japanese which makes him, within a U.S. context, mixed race. See Schmitz 2015.

14 Holtzclaw was convicted on eighteen of the thirty-six charges against him and sentenced to 263 years in prison.

15 The apparent intensification of self-blame for impaired and incapacitated victims points to a limitation of Heyes's important and overall astute analysis. One is not blamed for falling asleep and thus assaults of sleeping victims are viewed more sympathetically than those of victims who have consumed alcohol or other substances.

16 Findings by Littleton et al. support the idea that "given the strong stigma against heavy drinking among women," intoxicated victims are viewed as more blameworthy than victims who had not consumed alcohol. Their work also shows that internalized victim-blaming appears to be more acute in impaired and especially in incapacitated victims. In addition to engaging in the highest levels of self-blame, incapacitated victims are particularly susceptible to feelings of stigmatization that are unrelated to the external blame they actually experience. In other words, consistent with humiliation, it is the "victim's own perception of [their] experience" that generates "self-blame and . . . feelings of stigma" (see Littleton, Grills, and Axsom 2009).

17 Existential threat is also conveyed in a less extreme form in Bartky's account, where "mere words" can stop her in her tracks and humiliate her.

18 Racist constructions of Black women as the sexually promiscuous opposites of "virtuous" white women are clearly informed by white middle class norms that posit women as the gatekeepers of sex. One of the implications for Black women of being subjected to norms they can never fulfill is thus a contradictory and therefore particularly pernicious form of victim-blaming: when one can never be anything but responsible for one's sexual violation one cannot in effect be violated.

19 A recent *New York Times* article, "45 Stories of Sex and Consent on Campus," is instructive in this regard (see Bennet and Jones 2018).

20 Jessica Bennet's *New York Times* op-ed, 'When Saying "Yes" Is Easier Than Saying "No"' is instructive on this point (see Bennet 2017). It is important to note, again, that women of color are simultaneously held to the standards of and excluded from white middle class norms of feminine respectability.

21 Anna North (2018) provides insightful feminist analysis of the Ansari case.

3 Speaking out, countering sexual humiliation, transforming oneself

"Is it possible," Foucault queried in 1982, "to constitute, or reconstitute, an aesthetics of the self? At what cost and under what conditions" (2005, 251)? Foucault's concern here, and throughout his 1982 Collège de France course, *The Hermeneutics of the Subject*, is ethico-political self-fashioning: whether and how it is possible within a contemporary context to develop modes of self-constitution, -relation, and -understanding with the potential to counter normalizing power relations. Indeed, Foucault identifies the self-relation as both the "first" and "final point of resistance to political power" (252).

Foucault's questions are driven in part by what he sees as the ineffectual nature of current efforts toward cultivating counter-normalizing modes of self-relation. He characterizes prevailing conceptualizations of our relationship to ourselves as "almost" totally devoid of meaning, and he contends that we have nothing "to be proud of in our current efforts to reconstitute an ethic of the self" (2005, 251). "I think we may have to suspect," he observes, "that we find it impossible today to constitute an ethic of the self, even though it may be an urgent, fundamental, and politically indispensable task" (252). Despite his pessimism, Foucault did not simply pack up his lecture notes at this point and depart; rather, he dedicated two additional Collège courses to interrogating the possibilities he appears to deny. I think what he is trying to do here, then, is impress upon us the magnitude and implications of our failures thus far and, therefore, to instill in us the sense of urgency he felt toward proceeding along different lines.

Foucault's 1983 and 1984 Collège courses analyze the practice of *parrhēsia*, a broad definition of which is truth-telling or "free-spokenness" (*franc parler*). Foucault presents *parrhēsia* as a distinctively oppositional practice. In both its political (as a mode of speech) and ethical (as a mode of existence) forms, *parrhēsia* reveals, confronts, and facilitates the countering of oppression and injustice. Of particular interest to Foucault is the mode of self-constitution, -understanding, and -relation, that *parrhēsia* both reflects and engenders. Practitioners of *parrhēsia* constitute a relationship to themselves in and through the truth, but they do so in a manner that directly and overtly opposes the obedience, conformity, and perpetual self-renunciation that characterize a confessional mode of self-relation. The link Foucault draws between the confessional self-relation and subjectivity, together with his identification of the self-relation as the locus of both normalization and its countering, points to a view of *parrhēsia* as producing effects within a historical context that, were they produced by contemporary practices, would possess counter-normalizing potential.

Pointing to this potential is not to say that *parrhēsia* can or should be practiced today. As I see it, Foucault is not offering *parrhēsia* as a historical solution to contemporary problems. An ancient ethics of the self cannot be reconstituted within a contemporary and therefore completely different socio-historical context. Rather, and consistent with his criticism of our heretofore "blocked and ossified" efforts (as well as his use of the qualifier "may" in his expression of dubiousness), Foucault is challenging us to create our own counter-normalizing modes of self-relation and other/world relations that are able to respond to the idiosyncrasies of normalization in our time (2005, 251). This challenge entails identifying contemporary practices that reflect and therefore also have the potential to promote at least aspects of the kind of counter-normalizing self-relation reflected in *parrhēsia*; critically analyzing those practices in order to more fully understand the conditions from which they emerge; and cultivating conditions under which a plurality of counter-normalizing modes of existence may proliferate.

The next two chapters take up Foucault's challenge. In what follows, I turn to his 1983 Collège course, *The Government of Self and Others*, in order to analyze political *parrhēsia* and argue that analogous contemporary practices and modes of self-relation can facilitate feminist countering of sexual violence and humiliation; Chapter 4 provides a parallel treatment of ethical *parrhēsia*. Following its elucidation of political *parrhēsia*, the current chapter considers three instances of women speaking publicly in ways that reveal and confront the source of sexual violence and humiliation; the first instance entails legal testimony, whereas the other two entail forms of anti-sexual violence protest. Each of these modes of speaking reflects defining features of political *parrhēsia*, among the most important of which for my purposes is that they afford speakers the possibility of experiencing their relationship to themselves differently, in a way not characterized by the normalizing effects of subjectivity upon which sexual humiliation hinges. Having shown that cultivating contemporary modes of counter-normalizing/counter-humiliating self-relation is possible and identified some conditions under which it occurs, I conclude by considering at what cost the speakers in question risk their own ontological status and thus loosen their attachments to subjectivity.

I

Parrhēsia, according to Foucault, was exercised throughout antiquity, with its form and meaning varying according to place and time.[1] Despite this lack of uniformity, and admittedly scant textual records, Foucault elucidates some defining characteristics of political *parrhēsia*. A text written by Plutarch "almost exactly mid-way between the classical" and early Christian periods focuses on the *parrhēsia* of Dion, the brother-in-law of Dionysus I, "tyrant of Syracuse" (Foucault 2010, 46; 48). Under the tutelage of Plato, Dion was able to overcome his subservience to Dionysus and, believing the tyrant would benefit from Plato's instruction, Dion arranged for the two to meet. Plato's criticism of tyranny, however, angered Dionysus to the point that he endeavored to have Plato killed or, failing that, sold into slavery. Foucault relates that while Dionysus did not tolerate Plato's *parrhēsia*, he did so in the case of Dion, whom Dionysus "allowed to speak his mind boldly" (49).

Plato's and Dion's speech is recognizable as *parrhēsia*, Foucault argues, on the basis neither of its discursive forms or strategies nor (at least not fully) its content. While *parrhēsia* opposes flattery (which is simply untruthful), it may make use of but is not reducible to demonstration, rhetoric, pedagogy, or debate, and it departs most dramatically from the latter two. In contrast to pedagogy, which entails a gradual progression toward the truth, the parrhesiast "throws the truth in the face of the person" it addresses (Foucault 2010, 54). This "abrupt," even "violent" manner of confronting someone with the truth prevents debate: it leaves the one confronted unable to respond, at least discursively (54; 55). As is the case with Dionysus, who could respond to Plato only through vengeful action, *parrhēsia* either forces those it confronts to respond on a "different register," leaves them "choked with fury," or simply renders them "silent" (54).

The distinguishing feature of *parrhēsia* is that the content of what is said is articulated from a particular stance or attitude exhibited by the speaker; it is expressed by, as well as the expression of, a particular mode of self-relation. This self-relation is a product of and itself reproduces conditions, as seen in the situations of Dion and (especially) Plato, that expose the speaker to "unspecified" risk, up to and including "their own death" (Foucault 2010, 56). Speaking the truth under such conditions produces a "doubling effect": it creates a self-reflexive bond between speaker and truth; Foucault refers to it as a "pact of the speaking subject with himself" (64). Taking on the risks associated with doing so, the parrhesiast constitutes as well as understands and relates to themself as "the person who tells the truth, who has told the truth, and who recognizes [themself] in and as the person who has told the truth" (68).

Foucault further elucidates how *parrhēsia* affects, and what the practice in turn conveys concerning, the parrhesiast's "mode of being" by contrasting it with performative speech acts (2010, 68). The first point of difference he identifies is that performative speech acts are "codified" such that their effects are both predictable and readily intelligible. A judge's pronouncement, "you are now married," has the same ramifications for any two individuals standing before them. *Parrhēsia*'s pronouncements, by contrast, occur under conditions characterized by uncertainty, the specific effects of which cannot be anticipated and which, as previously noted, expose the speaker to potentially dire risk. A second point of difference concerns the speaker's status, which is definitive in a performative utterance. It is because *a judge* utters the words, "You are now married" that two individuals become a wed couple. Third, and related, the judge's status is unaffected by their actual relationship to the words they utter (i.e., whether or not the judge thinks the law is valid). The situation with *parrhēsia* is completely different. The parrhesiast's status is irrelevant (both Plato the philosopher and Dion the brother-in-law practice *parrhēsia*), while their relationship to what they say, as noted, is crucial. Because the simultaneous binding of self to self and self to truth that occurs in *parrhēsia* is not an effect of the speaker's status, it is not requisite; Plato and Dion *willingly* forge and constitute themselves in terms of this self-reflexive pact. Insofar as it is neither generated from nor delimited by predetermined institutional norms, moreover, the speech of Plato and Dion, and hence the respective self-relations it reflects, is characterized by freedom. Rather than reproducing the same set of predetermined conditions necessary for the (re)validation of the speaker's existing self-relation and the same set of codified outcomes, as an "irruptive truth-telling," *parrhēsia* reproduces uncertainty and risk both generally and in terms of the speaker's relationship to themself. In short, *parrhēsia* is (self)transformative. It reflects and cultivates the speaker's capacity to become other than what they currently are, but does not dictate the nature of such transformation. In light of this uncertain and potentially dire risk, Foucault identifies courage as being "at the heart of *parrhēsia*" (66).

Foucault shows that political *parrhēsia* may take a variety of forms. Plato and Dion are advisors privately offering advice to a ruler. A second form, speaking publicly as a citizen in matters relating to state administration, figures centrally in Euripides' play, *Ion*, which Foucault analyzes across several lectures. That analysis further identifies two additional modes of political *parrhēsia* that are particularly significant, given Foucault's sustained interest in elucidating the relationship between truth, subjectivity, and power (2010, 154). In the first mode, an individual tells someone with whom they have a close personal relationship about a wrong they have committed. In the second, an individual of lower sociopolitical stature confronts a powerful person who has committed an injustice against them. The dynamics of confession are clearly apparent in the first (confessional *parrhēsia*), whereas the second (judicial *parrhēsia*) more directly reflects the general characteristics of political *parrhēsia* outlined above.

The speaker of what Foucault identifies as paradigmatic confessional and judicial *parrhēsia* is Ion's mother, Creusa. Ion was conceived when the god Apollo raped Creusa, who never disclosed that she had been attacked, hid her pregnancy, and subsequently abandoned Ion after giving birth. Unbeknownst to Creusa, Ion was rescued (by Hermes at Apollo's order) and became a servant in Apollo's temple. An oracle Apollo delivers years later to Creusa's husband, Xuthus, leads him (Xuthus) to believe that Ion is his son.

This is an unfortunate turn of events for Creusa, who does not know that Ion is in fact the child she left to die: Ion will inherit Xuthus's wealth while she, like all childless women in "noble" families, will be sent off to live a solitary life (Foucault 2010, 118). Foucault thus describes Creusa as suffering a "double injustice" at Apollo's hands: he raped her, and his oracle threatens her future well-being (108).[2] It is with respect to the second injustice that Creusa engages in confessional *parrhēsia*, revealing to her elderly tutor (with whom she is in fact conspiring to kill Ion) that she had a son whom she abandoned (an action which subsequently, she believes, resulted in her current predicament). With respect to Apollo's first injustice against her, Creusa engages in judicial *parrhēsia*. She confronts Apollo about the fact that he raped her and the events his oracle has put into motion: "Oh! What wretched souls we women are! Oh! The crimes of the gods! Where shall we go to demand justice when it is the iniquity of the powerful that destroys us?" (134–135).

Creusa's speech exhibits the general characteristics of political *parrhēsia*, as well as those of judicial *parrhēsia* more specifically. She publicly ("in front of everyone, in broad daylight"), overtly and directly confronts Apollo with the injustices he has committed (Foucault 2010, 133). Insofar as Creusa's speech is not legitimized by any social, political, or institutional status (consistent with judicial *parrhēsia*, this lack of status and legitimation is conspicuous), in confronting Apollo, she exposes herself to risk, the extent of which she cannot anticipate. This lack of institutional legitimation and, therefore, protection reflects the free and courageous nature of Creusa's speech. It is free in both the sense that it is not requisite and in the sense that insofar as it stems from, opens onto, and thus confronts uncertainty it transforms Creusa the speaker in equally unanticipated ways. In publicly speaking the truth (women are violated by those in power and when this happens they have nowhere to turn), Creusa thus binds herself to it, constituting, understanding, and relating to herself as a truth-teller. "What can we do," Foucault asks,

> when the iniquity of the powerful destroys us and we must demand justice? We can do precisely what Creusa does . . . at risk and danger to [ourselves] . . . stand up before the person who committed the injustice and speak.
>
> (134; 135)

The examples of Plato and Dion, and especially of Creusa, illustrate that political *parrhēsia* is an oppositional practice: all three speakers confront and expose unjust exercises of power. Despite important points of intersection between the two practices, this oppositional character marks a radical point of departure between *parrhēsia* and confession. On the one hand, both *parrhēsia* and confession are verbal practices of truth-telling. In *parrhēsia*, as in confession, one "tell[s] all"; "nothing of the truth" is "hidden" or withheld (Foucault 2011, 10). Moreover, both confession and *parrhēsia* forge a relation of self to self in and through forging a relationship to the truth. The characteristics of these respective self-relations, on the other hand, diverge sharply. As I showed in Chapter 1, a confessional mode of self-relation is defined by an internal, strongly negative, and elusive aspect that generates an anxious self-reflexive uncertainty. Verbally expressing to another person the state of one's soul as reflected in the particular and unique content of one's thoughts ostensibly counters that uncertainty by making manifest the speaker's (internal) truth. The dynamic nature of thoughts necessitates their continual expression, thereby permanently linking the manifestation of truth with an obligation to obey and to speak.

In light of this permanent obligation to speak, externalization might appear to be an additional, crucial shared characteristic of confession and *parrhēsia*. Both practices externalize the truth of the speaker. In confession, this is a pre-existing, fixed truth; externalization makes manifest what already exists and will not change. Because what exists is at the same time elusive and negative, externalization plays a key role in establishing a self-relation in which the assertion of self is always at the same time a self-negation: it facilitates the simultaneous intensification and masking of the interconnection between truth and uncertainty. As a tool of self-decipherment, moreover, in confession externalization is ultimately and paradoxically directed back toward the speaker. In *parrhēsia*, by contrast, externalization continually unfolds outward into the world. Because one risks oneself in speaking the truth, constituting oneself in terms of having done so entails a self-investment in or -commitment to becoming otherwise; self-constitution is an ongoing self-transformation. That the parrhesiastic self-relation attaches to itself through a loosening of attachments – that it is a self-relation that is simultaneously a self-undoing – emerges from the uncertainty and risk (re)produced by the oppositional nature of the truth the parrhesiast articulates. *Parrhēsia*'s "irruption of true discourse," Foucault attests, "opens the situation and makes possible effects which are, precisely, not known" (2010, 62). The parrhesiastic self-relation thus promotes not disavowal and masking of uncertainty and its accompanying risk, but critical and creative engagement with both that reflects and in turn cultivates freedom and courage. Indeed, Foucault locates freedom's "highest exercise" in the self-reflexive pact with truth that characterizes the parrhesiastic self-relation (67).

Foucault's presentation of *parrhēsia* as a kind of counter-confession has important implications for thinking about counter-normalizing and counter-humiliating interventions within a contemporary context. Externalizing practices that open onto rather than foreclose open-ended potentiality, and which are characterized by risk, self-transformation, freedom, courage, and critique and creativity generally, directly oppose the internalization, obedience, and conformity that subjectivity inherits from a confessional mode of self-relation. This experience of an alternative way of constituting, understanding, and relating to ourselves loosens attachments to subjectivity. It is a moment in which attachment to constraint, and of being constrained in those attachments, can be recognized. As discussed in Chapter 2, this subversively transformative moment opens onto broader opposition, critique, and resistance. Ongoing redirection of critical and creative capacities in new and unpredictable ways generates practices and modes of self-relation with the potential to disrupt normalizing self-relation and other/world relations. Rather than reproducing and therefore bolstering current limits and constraints, such practices and modes are constrained only by the need to continually confront constraint; they therefore undermine the experience of constraint as enablement inculcated by both subjectivity itself, and its uncritical acceptance as the only possible mode of self-relation. To engage in counter-normalization is therefore to risk the suspension of one's ontological status. As Foucault's analysis of *parrhēsia* makes clear and as Butler asserts continues to be the case, through undertaking this risk it becomes possible to "live in . . . less constrained way[s]" (Butler 2004, 192).

That a rape victim is the most prominent parrhesiast in Foucault's analysis has important implications for thinking about, more specifically, how ontologically risky practices and modes of self-relation can further feminist countering of sexual violence and humiliation. Foucault describes Creusa as not only having experienced a double injustice, but as speaking from a "position of double humiliation" (2010, 120). Insofar as one of the sources of this humiliation is rape, Creusa's *parrhēsia* emanates from a position of sexual humiliation. That Creusa was viewed as subhuman is apparent in gendered relations of power according to which, as an ostensibly childless wife, Creusa faced banishment when it appeared as if Ion were Xuthus's son. Such treatment indicates that women were stigmatized – effectively reduced to their biological, embodied reproductive capacities and, therefore, not viewed as beings possessing the capacity for freedom. Apollo treated Creusa as if she were nonhuman when he raped her. Abandoning Ion in an attempt to hide the fact that she had been raped, as well as her confessional *parrhēsia*, imply self-blame that reflects Creusa's internalization of her treatment. Given that Creusa's judicial *parrhēsia* thus emerges not only from humiliating conditions but also from the actual experience of sexual humiliation, it is all the more compelling from a feminist perspective. When she speaks the truth of her sexual humiliation, she constitutes herself in terms of it; put differently, the experience of that humiliation is constitutive of the pact she forges with herself as parrhesiast. At the same time, the risk Creusa undertakes and the uncertainty it generates makes this self-constitutive speaking of the truth externalizing in a manner that is simultaneously self-transformative. Stemming from and in turn promoting courage and freedom, Creusa's assertion of her existing relationship to herself at the same time enacts her becoming other than what she currently is. Insofar as the sexual humiliation she experienced does not circle back onto her as speaker, the mode of self-relation it reflects can be distinguished not only from a confessional mode, which would retain humiliation as central to who she is by (perpetually) reproducing it through its renunciation, but also from a defensive mode of self-relation that endeavors to (perpetually) deflect humiliation. Creusa's "turning back against Apollo a truth he knows full well" points to a different sort of doubling than those Foucault identifies (121). This movement entails an experience of humiliation that simultaneously confronts its source and exposes it precisely in its inhumanity and injustice. It is an experience of humiliation that is simultaneously an experience of its countering, of an exposure that also exposes. Rather than being directed back toward and therefore redoubled within the speaker, the experience of humiliation is directed outward as critique.

Creusa's practice of judicial *parrhēsia* and the self-relation it reflects offer insight into characteristics of contemporary practices and modes of self-relation that are able to mark sexual violence and humiliation as significant harms without making them definitive of either women's relationship to themselves or their situation in the world. The example of Creusa shows, in other words, that it is possible to acknowledge and even experience the harm of sexual violation without internalizing and therefore perpetually reproducing it. Ontologically risky practices that direct humiliation outward by means of publicly, assertively, or even aggressively confronting its source disrupt the internalization upon which humiliation hinges. Such practices inhibit the turning back of critical and creative capacities onto themselves in ways that foreclose freedom; as perilous and uncertain, moreover, they entail continued deployment of critique and creativity and, therefore, of freedom and courage. Ontologically risky practices therefore inhibit the formation of a self-renouncing, obedient, and conformist self-relation that views and experiences itself as unworthy of being otherwise. Crucially, risking one's own ontological status disrupts the cycle of self-assertion and -renunciation that threatens to produce a self-relation of domination unable to resist and counter normalizing power relations more broadly. In Foucauldian terms, ontological risk presents us with an opportunity that is also a "task."[3] As I shall make clear, the cultivation of counter-normalizing and counter-humiliating modes of self-relation and other/world relations is not a release from norms, structures, and institutions that produce and legitimize sexual violence and humiliation, any more than practicing *parrhēsia* frees Creusa from the gendered constraints of ancient Greek society. Creusa confronts Apollo from within the context that allowed the violation of rape to occur, but she does so from a stance that exposes and challenge sources and conditions for the possibility of sexual violence. Similarly, ontologically risky modes of self-relation that subvert the individuating and negating exposure and display of sexual humiliation are generated within but neither merely replicate nor uncritically support nor reproduce normalizing gendered relations of power. More broadly, then, ontological risk creates an opening toward navigating relations of power in ways that open and expand them, fostering development and encouraging direction of critical and creative capacities in oppositional ways.

II

Analyzing concrete instances in which victims/survivors speak out against specific sources of sexual violence and sexual humiliation, as well as the conditions for their possibility, elucidates the counter-normalizing potential of ontologically risky practices and modes of self-relation, as well as their more specific relevance for countering sexual violence and sexual humiliation. All three instances of ontologically risky speech I consider take the form of the disempowered confronting the empowered who have harmed them. In each instance, moreover, disempowerment is reflected in conditions of precarity that license, legitimize, and (albeit in diverse ways and to differing degrees) intensify the effects of speakers being viewed as subhuman, thereby facilitating their individual treatment as if they were nonhuman. Considering different types of speech made by differently-positioned women within various sociohistorical and institutional contexts provides insight into a variety of manifestations and effects of ontological risk. As my elucidation of the effects on the self-relation of practicing ontologically risky speech shows, this is at the same time insight into normalizing power – the degree to which it may become entrenched and intransigent, and thus by extension the complicated and frequently fraught nature of its countering. Ultimately, this analysis shows that it is indeed possible within a contemporary context to constitute a counter-normalizing/counter-humiliating mode of self-relation, and it provides a sense of the cost associated with taking on the risk of doing so.

Having previously illustrated that Daniel Holtzclaw's victims were subjected to sexual humiliation, here I show that their testimony against Holtzclaw constitutes an ontologically risky, counter-normalizing/counter-humiliating practice. To the extent that the testimony provided by Holtzclaw's victims reflects norms that shape and govern legal proceedings, it is codified speech. That testimony does not, however, merely reflect such norms; indeed, in important respects, it calls them into question by exposing their normalizing character. As I showed in Chapter 2, within a context of systemic, institutionalized racism, discrediting or ignoring people of color who publicly express the truth of their experiences upholds normalizing (racist) power relations. Black women, predominantly poor, doing so in order to hold a man accountable for acts of sexual violence he committed against them while he was a police officer thereby exposes and interrupts the seamless reproduction of the normative and normalizing racism of the legal system. Even as it gets articulated in and through legal norms, Holtzclaw's victims' testimony stands in opposition to them. Precisely as oppositional, that testimony can be seen as an ontologically risky practice. As a threat to the institution within which it gets produced, the victims'/survivors' speech lacks institutional legitimation and therefore puts them at risk. That risk took a variety of forms. Some victims/survivors indicated that they did not report being raped and assaulted not only because they did not think the police would believe them, but also because they feared police retaliation (Testa 2015). One victim/survivor was cautioned by a friend that disclosing what Holtzclaw had done to her might result in retaliation within her own community. "I was afraid," she related, "of what could happen to me if I did snitch or if people around my neighborhood thought I was snitching or talking to the police" (Ibid). Victims/survivors also risked and in fact faced further humiliation. The same dynamic that reduced the women to the conditions of their precarity and thus facilitated, legitimized, and subsequently masked the harm of their sexual violation cast them not only as "imperfect victims," but also as both unreliable witnesses and speakers of untruths. This reductive framing, which reflects a perception of the women as subhuman and opens onto their nonhuman treatment, was overtly invoked by Holtzclaw's defense during the trial, and he has since taken it up himself (Hernandez 2016; Redden and Gambino 2015). It is also implicit in the dearth of media attention to the case, the meager attendance at Holtzclaw's trial, and the lack of expressions of support from white feminist organizations for his victims. Grace E. Franklin, member of OKC (Oklahoma City) Artists for Justice, an organization that stood in solidarity with the victims/survivors throughout, asked, "Why aren't there more women out here of all shades, of all backgrounds for these women? Why are we doing this alone?" (Lussenhop 2015).

Like the legal testimony of the victims/survivors in the Holtzclaw case, the Brown University "Rape List" opposed the institution within which it emerged. When the story of "the List" broke in the national media in 1990, Brown's student code of conduct did not include rape and sexual assault as violations. The practice at that time was to handle reports of sexual violence through an informal "mediation" process (Jucliu 2008a). Outcomes of that process included requiring accused men to write notes of apology to accusers, having the men's actions reported to their sports team coaches, and men being required to run extra laps during sports practices (Ibid). Given that reporting was ineffectual, women students began communicating in writing on the bathroom walls of the university's Rockefeller Library (aka, "the Rock") in order to identify and warn one another away from perpetrators. The communication was, then, a "conversation" rather than simply a list of names. According to Jesselyn Brown-Radack, who was sexually assaulted during her sophomore year at Brown, women had been using "the Rock wall" in this way "for years" (Ibid).[4]

Each time custodial staff, at the direction of the administration, removed the writing, the students duly reproduced it.[5] Perceiving that Brown's administration was more concerned with protecting men's reputations than with women's sexual violation, women students' frustration and anger increased and spread, with new conversations emerging on the walls of restrooms in other campus buildings. After the student newspaper, *The Brown Daily Herald*, published a story about "the List," men students began expressing concern that their names might appear, or outrage at having been accused. At a subsequent forum on sexual harassment, women students angrily confronted the administrators who were present and also staged a silent protest in which one of them stood up every three minutes and remained standing for the forum's duration in order to symbolize the frequency at which rape occurred against U.S. women (Celis 1990; Raman 2004).[6] On November 18, the *New York Times* ran a story about the situation at Brown (Celis 1990). On November 29, Phil Donahue dedicated his show to discussing it; Jesselyn Brown (later Brown-Radack), along with Lisa Billowitz, Jenn David, and Christin Lahiff, who had also taken prominent roles in pushing Brown's administration to act, as well as Toby Simon, Assistant Dean and Director of Health Education, participated. In response to the media attention, Brown's president issued a statement in which he promised "swift" development of a university sexual misconduct policy (Raman 2004).

Women students at Brown confronted unjust power by means of the bathroom wall communication, the sexual harassment forum, and the appearance on *Donahue*. That they did so from a disempowered position is apparent in the conditions of humiliation to which they were subjected. Victims of sexual violence were ignored, discouraged, belittled, as well as simply not believed when they reported what had happened to them. This trivialization of sexual violence reflects and reproduces gendered relations of power that view women as subhuman. The students' inability to gain recognition for and therefore validation of the harm they experienced reflects a view of women as beings lacking the capacity to (fully) experience and therefore (fully) express human states in (fully) human ways; insofar as this is the case they are treated as less than (fully) injurable.[7] Being subjected to sexual violence is of course to be treated as if nonhuman.

Given that Brown's trivialization of sexual violence against its students reflects a view of women as subhuman that resulted in and legitimized their treatment as if nonhuman, the speech of the students' protest can be seen as emerging within and in response to conditions for the possibility of sexual humiliation. That protesting speech publicly, assertively, and sometimes aggressively expressed the truth of women's experiences of rape, sexual assault, and disenfranchisement. Administrators were unable to respond discursively to the students' protest; ultimately, the university responded through action by formulating and implementing a sexual misconduct policy. Given that Brown administrators perceived the students' protest as a potential threat to the integrity of the university, that protest speech was without institutional legitimacy and therefore placed the students at indeterminate risk. Like the victims/survivors in the Holtzclaw case, the students risked retaliation and further humiliation. Being identified as authors of the bathroom wall communication could have resulted in disciplinary action for defacing university property. Angry men students created a "counter-list of women who need to be raped" (Liu and Klayman 2014). Brown's administration once again expressed more concern about protecting the rights of men who had been named as perpetrators than about countering sexual violence and addressing the needs of victims. Named men received a letter informing them that deans were available for counseling and that the men could file a complaint if they wished to do so; administrators disparagingly referred to women students as "magic marker terrorists" (Jucliu 2008b).

Ontologically risky anti-sexual violence protest speech is also apparent in the contemporary phenomenon of #MeToo. In her work with young victims/survivors of color, activist Tarana Burke developed the idea of using the phrase "Me Too" as a means of disclosing experiences of sexual violence that would convey (1) that the individual who is disclosing is not alone but rather part of a broader and supportive community of victims/survivors and (2) that sexual violence is a widespread problem.[8] #MeToo is thus a particular appropriation and deployment of Burke's activism that, as I see it (and as I shall discuss), effectively conveys the latter issue but falls short relative to the former. Whereas Burke has been employing "MeToo" for years, #MeToo emerged in October of 2017. On October 5, the *New York Times* broke the story that media mogul Harvey Weinstein had been committing acts of sexual violence against numerous women for years.[9] In response to the "suggestion" that doing so would "give people a sense of the magnitude of the problem," on October 15, actress Alyssa Milano sent out her tweet asking women and men who had experienced sexual violence to respond "me too."[10] The overwhelming number of responses generated momentum behind the emergence and expansion of #MeToo, as more women made accusations against an increasing number of prominent men in fields such as media and politics.

As with the victims/survivors in the Holtzclaw case and the Brown students, the disempowerment of #MeToo speakers is apparent in both their sexual violation and the absence or ineffectual nature of available structures for reporting. Many women who have attempted to report experiences of sexual violence have had to deal with responses ranging from ignorance to disbelief to hostility. Refusing to take women at their word and to therefore take sexual violence seriously reflects and reproduces women's normative subhumanization. The variety of (and in many cases multiple) forms of sexual violence, from sexual harassment to rape, #MeToo speakers have experienced reflects their treatment as if they were nonhuman. Whether accusers remain within or have left the institutions in which they were abused, insofar as it challenges influential institutional figures #MeToo speech threatens the institutions themselves and is therefore not legitimized by them. Speaking out thus puts speakers at indeterminate risk.

Given the diversity of individuals, contexts, and institutions implicated by an equally diverse array of #MeToo speakers, risk has manifested in a wide variety of ways, among these (and again consistent with the Holtzclaw case and Brown) are retaliation and further humiliation. Weinstein reportedly overtly threatened his victims with physical violence as well as other forms of retaliation if they told anyone (let alone officially reported) what he had done to them. Moira Donegan, who started the "Shitty Media Men" list, was fired when the list was made public.[11] Donegan's list, while it was compiled in a Google spreadsheet, bears marked resemblances to the Brown bathroom wall conversations. Frustrated and angry in the face of unacknowledged systemic misogyny within her profession, Donegan created and circulated the document as a way for woman working in the media to anonymously identify and inform one another about predatory men. After the list was "exposed," Donegan writes, "my life changed dramatically. I lost friends . . . I lost my job . . . I've learned that protecting women is a position that comes with few protections itself" (Donegan 2018). When Helen Donahue reported a company executive at Vice Media for groping her at a holiday party, she was told by the company's human resources department that it was not harassment – he was simply "making a move on her" (Kantor 2018). Having disclosed her experience to the *New York Times* in 2017, several months later, Donahue told that newspaper in a follow-up story that she feels "more isolated" as well as more anxious "since speaking out." The article, Donahue explains, "strained several of [her] remaining relationships with people in media;" she states that she now refrains from having "even moderately close relationships with co-workers" (Ibid). Drew Dixon, one of several women who has brought rape charges against media mogul Russell Simmons, describes the difficult position in which Black women who have accused Black men find themselves.[12] Having, like Donahue, told her story in the *Times*, Dixon relates that she felt like a "weight had been lifted from [her] shoulders" when the article was published. At the same time, she also felt conflicted. "It's very hard as a black woman to call out powerful black men," she states, "because we have no heroes to spare. We are always . . . trying to overcome this myth of the predatory black man" (Ibid).

Self-blame, I have suggested, can be seen to reflect internalization of external perspectives and therefore, by extension, the experience of humiliation on the part of victims/survivors. I have pointed to evidence of self-blame in some of Holtzclaw's victims; it is also suggested in Helen Donahue's account above, as well as in accounts of other #MeToo speakers I shall discuss below. Because available information about Brown, including interviews with the four women who as students appeared on the *Donahue* show, focuses on the situation at the university and the students' protest rather than on the experiences of women who were raped and sexually assaulted, it's not possible to make a determination about the experience of sexual humiliation by victims/survivors within that context. What my analysis of the Holtzclaw case and the Brown and #MeToo protests clearly shows, however, is that victims/survivors in each instance were *subjected to* sexual humiliation. Each of these instances reflects the normative view of women as subhuman, as well as the treatment as if nonhuman this view facilitates. Not only was women's sexual violation facilitated and legitimized, the harm of such violation was minimized – both when it occurred and when women spoke out publicly about their experiences.

Like Creusa, victims/survivors in the Holtzclaw case, at Brown, and within the context of #MeToo, can therefore all be seen as speaking from a position of double humiliation. Their ontologically risky speech, like her confrontation of Apollo, moreover, possesses counter-normalizing and counter-humiliating potential. Victims/survivors spoke publicly; given that their speech challenged the institutions within which it was generated, it was not institutionally legitimated. As the victim-blaming and trivialization of sexual violence these women experienced illustrate, in publicly confronting the source of their sexual humiliation they exposed themselves to risk, the nature and extent of which they could not anticipate and which in many cases still remain to be seen. Their speech thus not only reflects and generates uncertainty, it also engages it. And it is in this engagement that possibilities for self-transformation are located. In speaking the truth of their sexual violation and sexual humiliation, these victims/survivors forge a pact with and thus a relationship to themselves in and through that truth and, hence, through that violation and humiliation – not by internalizing and permanently constituting themselves in terms of them, but rather by turning sexual humiliation back against its source and thus externalizing it in a way that reverberates outward rather than redoubling back toward them as speakers. The self-exposure that occurs in these victims'/survivors' ontologically risky speech does not, therefore, reassert and entrench subhumanity and sexual humiliation and their requisite perpetual self-renunciation. It reveals constraint in self-attachment, facilitates loosening of that attachment in the form of self-critique, disrupts the formation of a self-relation of abjection, and opens onto possibilities for alternative modes of self-relation.

Simply put, the moment in which Holtzclaw's victims, the Brown students, and #MeToo speakers confronted the sources of sexual humiliation was a singular experience of difference – an experience, that is, of their becoming other to themselves. These women can draw upon and expand this experience in the ongoing cultivation of their relationship to themselves; given the interconnection of self-relation and other/world relations, their experience possesses broader transformative potential as well. That this cultivation engages and therefore reproduces both uncertainty and risk, and that it takes place, moreover, within the context of normalizing power makes clear that there are no guarantees about the nature of the transformation that takes place. When we constitute ourselves in terms of uncertainty and risk, we reproduce them; hence, the ongoing challenge to navigate relations of power such that possibilities created by this uncertainty and risk maximize enablement and minimize constraint. In the face of not only the absence but the impossibility of being able to anticipate the effects of efforts toward counter-normalization, there will always be a cost associated with the ontological risk it entails. Part of this cost is the normalizing effects of our own potentially counter-normalizing practices and modes of self-relation.

III

The three instances of ontologically risky speech I have considered did certainly produce counter-normalizing effects. Holtzclaw was convicted and sentenced to spend the rest of his life in prison. The lack of support for his victims ended up generating new local and broader forms of activism. OKC Artists for Justice formed for the specific purpose of supporting Holtzclaw's victims and drawing attention to the case. Activist groups associated with the broader Black Lives Matter movement came to Oklahoma City to stand with local groups and the victims/survivors. In the absence of traditional media coverage of the case, activists created new Twitter hashtags: #SayHerName, #BlackWomenMatter, #Visible4Justice, #StandWithHer and #OKC13. The students at Brown succeeded in getting a sexual misconduct policy established. They also brought national attention to the issue of campus sexual violence and inspired student activists in subsequent generations. #MeToo, Catharine MacKinnon asserts, has accomplished what normative legal structures and institutions "could not" (2018). Weinstein has been arrested and is awaiting trial on charges of first- and third-degree rape, as well as "first-degree criminal sex act" (McKinley 2018). Other prominent men within the entertainment industry have been fired from their jobs; politicians have resigned. *Time* magazine bestowed its 2017 Person of the Year award upon the women of #MeToo, whom it dubbed "The Silence Breakers" (Zacharek, Dockterman, and Edwards 2017).

How is normalization, and therefore increased constraint, apparent within these counter-normalizing developments? With respect to the Holtzclaw case, normalizing potential is apparent in Jannie Ligons' portrayal, one might even say deployment, by the media and prosecution. The fact that Ligons did not reside in the same low income neighborhood as the rest of Holtzclaw's victims and had neither an arrest record nor substance abuse problems lent her a degree of what Iris Marion Young refers to as "respectability" (1990). Within a contemporary context, Young argues, norms of respectability primarily take the form of "professional comportment" characterized by embodied expressions of restraint including dress; grooming; and mannerisms, movement, and modes of speech (Ibid). The consistent framing of Ligons, both in the courtroom and more broadly, as "a fifty-seven-year-old grandmother" invokes respectability in ways that set her apart from the other victims, the bodies of whom are seen to reflect the disorder of the space in which they dwell. While respectability may have made Ligons a more credible speaker such that her reporting of Holtzclaw was able to ease the way for the rest of his victims to come forward, insofar as norms of respectability are characteristically white, middle-class, and masculine, invoking them subtly (or not so subtly) made Ligons a figure to whom whites generally (including the all-white jury) could more easily relate. Characterizing Ligons in this way therefore ultimately reasserted normative/normalizing raced/classed/gendered relations of power.

Both the Holtzclaw case and, as I implied earlier, the Brown protests point to the normalizing character of institutions. To the extent that institutions' primary interest is in sustaining and reproducing themselves, their normative structures, policies, and procedures, including those which ostensibly aim to prevent and alleviate harm, will ultimately be formulated in ways that protect the institutions rather than victims. As Catharine MacKinnon argues, formal legal protections can accomplish only so much in the face of practices, like sexual violence, that are legitimized and (re)asserted by the power relations that in turn shape institutions themselves. As normalizing institutions, law and academe both reflect and reproduce gendered/raced/classed conditions for the possibility of sexual violence. "If the same cultural inequalities are permitted to operate in law as in the behavior the law prohibits," MacKinnon writes, "equalizing attempts – such as sexual harassment law – will be systemically resisted" (2018). In pointing to how normalization manifests in multiple, complex, opaque, and entrenched ways, MacKinnon's remarks serve as a reminder that normalizing relations of power must be engaged on multiple fronts in an ongoing manner.

The myriad ways in which police and courts have furthered the precarity of people of color, the poor, and women, clearly illustrate that a counter-normalizing response to Holtzclaw's conviction cannot rely solely or ultimately on legal (or other) institutions. Such a response needs to include identification and analysis of broader conditions that made the conviction possible, as well as efforts toward cultivating similarly counter-normalizing/counter-humiliating conditions within other contexts. Noteworthy in regard to the normalizing character of institutions is the fact that Holtzclaw was not found guilty on all counts; his crimes against some victims were officially unacknowledged and, therefore, unrecognized. While the Brown students' 1990 protest elucidated the normalizing gendered relations of power and administrative structures at Brown, its normalizing effects (and aspects) are apparent in its narrow focus on achieving institutional change. Just as legislation hasn't eradicated sexual violence within society overall, neither have sexual misconduct policies prevented campus sexual violence or guaranteed positive outcomes for victims when it occurs. In the spring of 2014, a new "rape list" appeared on the Rock bathroom wall at Brown.[13] One again, women students had turned to informal communication in order to warn one another away from men who had committed rape or sexual assault but who nonetheless remained on campus.

The need for this speech, which both identifies and protests the inadequacy of Brown's sexual misconduct policy and administrative complacency in the face of it, is underscored by the case of Lena Sclove. In 2013, Sclove was raped by a fellow student (Liu and Klayman 2014). When she reported the incident, Sclove was "encouraged" by the university to have her case handled through the university's disciplinary process rather than going to the police. The university's process, Sclove relates, was presented at "more humane," "shorter," "less traumatic," and more "likely to keep

[her] in school and . . . on track to graduate" (Ibid). Sclove's assailant, Daniel Kopin, was ultimately "found responsible" for 'two counts of sexual misconduct and one count of using force that caused "physical harm"' and suspended from Brown for one year (McDonough 2014). Initially relieved at the outcome of the process, Sclove became distressed when she learned that Kopin would be returning to campus for her senior year. When her appeal of the decision allowing him to return was denied, Sclove publicly disclosed that she had been raped and how the university had responded.[14] As in 1990, protests broke out on Brown's campus, this time supporting Sclove and calling upon the university community to "Imagine Zero Rape" (Ibid).

According to anti-rape activist Sofie Karasek, "institutions seek to protect their bottom lines and insulate themselves from legal liability . . . it's not clear that they can ever be truly fair and unbiased" (2018). In Karasek's view, victims of campus sexual violence "need an option that is truly independent and, ideally, publicly funded."[15] Appealing to external bodies to address institutional problems could prove to be a positive intervention. At the same time, the normalizing effects of the 1990 Brown students' protest are not merely the result of a narrow focus on promoting change within the institution of the university. Normalization is also reflected in and reproduced by the race (and ostensibly) class privilege that would lead to such a focus: from a white privileged position, institutions work. As MacKinnon points out, and as the Brown women discovered, for white women this is of course not fully the case. But in virtue of their whiteness and attendance at an elite institution of higher education, the students were likely to have generally had the experience of institutions working for them; hence their perspective that Brown therefore ought or could be made to – or at the very least that the university could be prevented from working against them. This perspective contrasts starkly with that of Holtzclaw's victims, who identified and experienced institutions as not only ineffectual but in fact sources of increased precarity, humiliation, and oppression.

The normalizing effects of #MeToo further underscore the need for intersectional feminist anti-sexual violence practices. *Time*'s "Silence Breakers" feature opens with the following pronouncement:

> . . . [W]omen everywhere have begun to speak out about the inappropriate, abusive, and in some cases illegal behavior they've faced. When multiple harassment claims bring down a charmer like former *Today* show host Matt Lauer, women who thought they had no recourse see a new, wide-open door. When a movie star says #MeToo, it becomes easier to believe the cook who's been quietly enduring for years.
> (Zacharek, Dockterman, and Edwards 2017)

Actress Ashley Judd, the first woman to bring charges against Weinstein, states that since speaking out, she has "received waves of accolades and thanks;" moreover, "her longtime role as an activist has expanded" (Kantor

2018). "Now I want joyfully to shout from the rooftops, everyone come forward," Judd states.

> Everyone has to make their decision but I think we can safely say millions of others are here to offer support and hope. Nobody can do it for me, but I don't have to do it alone.
>
> (Ibid)

Judd's experience reflects the widely-held view that #MeToo had brought about radical, even unprecedented, positive change, as well as its characterization as a new kind of women's "movement." The experiences of many other #MeToo speakers, however, throw into sharp relief the privileged nature of both Judd's experience and her encouragement of all women to speak out on the basis of it. Experiences of working-class women, especially those of color, reveal the serious inaccuracy of *Time*'s general assertion that cooks and actresses are equally able to confront sources of sexual violence and humiliation. Indeed, *Time*'s own cover story illustrates that, as Sandra Pezqueda, one of the working-class women featured in "The Silence Breakers," puts it: "Someone who is in the limelight is able to speak out more easily than people who are poor. The reality of being a woman is the same – the difference is the risk each woman must take" (Zacharek, Dockterman, and Edwards 2017). Seven of the twenty-five accounts presented in the article are from working-class women.[16] That three of these seven are anonymous or partially so (in contrast to none of the accounts of white-collar women and public figures) reveals the intensified precarity of the condition of working-class women.[17]

Accounts from Black women workers at two Chicago Ford Motor Company plants, published in a 2017 *New York Times* article, are even more telling. In response to the largely white and privileged nature of #MeToo,[18] a former Ford employee initiated the #WhatAboutUs campaign in order to draw attention to treatment women workers at the company have been putting up with for decades: harassment that "has endured even though they work for a multinational corporation with a professional human resources operation . . . are members of one of the country's most powerful unions . . . a federal agency and then a federal judge sided with them, and . . . independent monitors policed the factory floors for several years" (Chira and Einhorn 2017). Women interviewed for the article describe daily harassment including "lewd comments," racial slurs, and remarks expressing hostility toward women for taking away "men's jobs," as well as a variety of forms of physical abuse: men rubbed their groins against women's bodies, grabbed their crotches and moaned when they looked at women, and exposed themselves. One woman related that she was coerced into having intercourse with her supervisor in order to get a work schedule adjustment that would allow her to secure childcare. Women who reported abusive men (to both Ford's human resources department and their own union) were brushed aside with comments like, "[Y]ou're a pretty woman, take it as a compliment," and "He only did it once. That's not sexual harassment"

(Ibid). They were also ostracized, threatened, and retaliated against. Suzette Wright left Ford in 2000 after the lawsuit in which she was a plaintiff was settled. "Each time that I was taking it," Wright explains, "it just felt like more of me was diminishing, just getting smaller until it was just like a shell of a person" (Ibid).

Since it emerged, I have experienced varying degrees of ambivalence about #MeToo, primarily because I worry that it has produced a normalizing obligation to speak. *Time*'s "Silence Breakers" feature reflects the contradictory nature of this obligation. Asserting that it is now safe to speak out and that anyone can do so implies that everyone *should*, even as the article's content undermines this assertion. I therefore also perceive in this obligation to speak an obligation to obey and hence an impetus toward the normalizing mode of self-relation of subjectivity. I see #MeToo speakers being defined in terms of their victimization; this reduction opens onto their defining themselves in the same way such that their externalization of the truth of sexual violence and humiliation ultimately rebounds, becomes self-constitutive, and therefore in need of perpetual renunciation. I also perceive normalizing effects in the fact that, Ashley Judd's opinion notwithstanding, many #MeToo speakers, the accounts of several of whom I have addressed, have not been supported. Not only is #MeToo potentially internalizing, then, thus far in my view it has been predominantly individual and therefore potentially individuating. It is for this reason that I have a hard time seeing it as a "movement."

IV

"It really does make my heart sink when I see it happening again, and kind of have to relive that and feel like we didn't make any difference," remarks Jesselyn Brown-Radack as she reflects upon Lena Sclove's case (Liu and Klayman 2014). Markedly similar sentiments are expressed by Sharon Dunn, who was part of a lawsuit women workers filed against Ford in the 1990s. "For all the good that was supposed to come out of what happened to us," Dunn relates, "it seems like Ford did nothing. If I had that choice today, I wouldn't say a damn word" (Chira and Einhorn 2017). Are Brown-Radack and Dunn correct? Are gains made by speaking out not worth the costs of doing so? Is ontologically risky speech generally and ontologically risky feminist protest speech more specifically merely ineffectual or even harmful? Would women be better off keeping silent and not putting their own ontological status, let alone their material and psychological well-being, at risk?

"I was incredibly naïve when I made the spreadsheet," reflects Moira Donegan.

> I thought the document would not be made public, and when it became clear that it would be, I was naïve because I thought the focus would be on the behavior described in the document, rather than on the document itself.

(2018)

After the Media Men list became public, a number of women disclosed to Donegan their experiences of being sexually violated; some told her that they had seen but not added the name of the man who attacked them to the list, an indication that he had victimized multiple women. Donegan states that in the face of anger – "not just at what happened to us but at the realization of the depth and frequency" of sexual harassment and violence – as well as anxiety about her own future, she nonetheless perceives a "[challenge] to imagine how we would prefer things to be" (Ibid). For her, this challenge is motivated not by "prescriptive dictation of acceptable sexual behaviors but the desire for a kinder, more respectful, and more equitable world" (Ibid). Donegan also points to the need to engage the challenge of identifying and cultivating the counter-normalizing potential within, rather than despairing at, a reality in which it is "still explosive, radical, and productively dangerous for women to say what we mean" (Ibid).

Suzette Wright describes life since talking to the *New York Times* about her experiences at Ford as "an emotional roller coaster." Speaking out, she explains, "resurfaced a lot of emotion . . . that was difficult to fish through" (Kantor 2018). As was the case for Donegan, readers of the article contacted Wright to share their own stories of harassment and abuse and to request her help. Given Wright's own emotional turmoil, she felt overwhelmed and "sought out mental health support. I knew I needed it to continue." At the same time, Wright asserts,

> I take every opportunity that comes my way because I know right now, in this moment, there are women who are still working in the plant and across other industries that are fearful of speaking . . . now the work has to happen.
>
> (Ibid)

I want to take away two points from Donegan's and Wright's accounts. First, both illustrate that within the context of normalizing relations of power, self-transformation cannot be construed in terms of a clean and simple increase in enablement and an accompanying reduction in constraint. That these two women were changed by their experiences is apparent in the fact that, as their accounts indicate, they have acquired new capacities. At the same time, as reflected in the emotional upheaval they describe, the change involved in this acquisition was deeply unsettling; as I have shown, it also came at a price. Donegan's and Wright's accounts illustrate the simultaneity of enablement and constraint. They show that counter-normalizing interventions themselves inevitably generate normalizing effects and, therefore, that part of counter-normalization is recognizing and grappling with the always limited and imperfect, and frequently fraught, nature of efforts toward creating conditions for the possibility of freedom and engaging in its practice. These two women's experiences also point to the need for thinking differently about the nature of positive transformation, about interventions that make a difference and those which fail to do so. At the level of the self-relation, "positive" transformation needs to entail movement toward increasing capacities that enable us to deal with a reality in which, as Foucault emphasizes, the work of freedom is an ongoing and fractious process – a reality in which, as Sara Ahmed reminds us, "[i]t is because we expose violence that we are heard as violent, as if the violence of which we speak originates with us" (2017, 253). Where not everything is bad but everything is indeed dangerous, positive transformation involves determining whether and when we are able to confront danger and expose violence and, if we are, which types and in what ways. It involves endeavoring to disentangle and wrestling with the ontological risks and costs of counter-normalization and the potential for domination inherent in normalization.

The second aspect of Donegan's and Wright's accounts to which I wish to draw attention is that both show that ontologically risky modes of self-relation are not merely individual, and that such modes therefore have the potential to manifest in ways that counter individuation. I find it instructive both that other women contacted Donegan and Wright after reading their accounts of their experiences, and that this reaching out was an unanticipated effect of Donegan's and Wright's public disclosure that in turn affected them in unanticipated ways. From a position of becoming otherwise to themselves, Donegan and Wright appeal to possibilities for broader transformation. Chapter 4 and especially Chapter 5 explore the potential of externalizing, counter-individuating practices and modes of self-relation to facilitate counter-normalizing/counter-humiliating, (self)transformative ways of connecting and coming together with others.

That the simultaneity of enablement and constraint leaves us, as Foucault puts it, in a "position of always beginning again" is discouraging only if we adhere to the need for certainty (1980c). The Holtzclaw case, the Brown protests, and #MeToo illustrate the depth, strength, and intransigence of patterns of inequality that form when the same relations of power are regenerated over and over again. The additional abuse and humiliation victims/survivors experienced as a result of speaking out underscores Foucault's point that confronting normalizing power entails potentially devastating risks that one can never anticipate and for which one can therefore never sufficiently prepare. Yet these instances of ontologically risky practice and self-relation also show that transformative intervention at the level of the self-relation reverberates in ways that can disrupt the seamless reproduction of prevailing relations of power. And this disruption creates an opportunity for something else to happen, for an experience of something different, for a loosening of (self)attachments. None of this may actually be taken up, or it can be taken up in ways that reinforce normalization. That is part of the risk which, if not taken, ensures nothing will happen other than what already is taking place. In the case of some victims/survivors, this could mean the reproduction of abjection, of a mode of relating to themselves as unworthy of anything other than subhumanity. Speaking out, then, ultimately reflects and generates possibilities for something else, possibilities without which there can be no emancipatory change.

I want to be clear that speaking publicly is *one way* of generating such possibility. Recall that it is our task to create and experiment with multiple ways of doing so. While the pervasiveness of normalization can be daunting, this very pervasiveness is its weak point, for it produces myriad opportunities for intervention and disruption. As Moira Donegan rightly observes, a context in which women simply speaking the truth is threatening to the point where it results in our characterization as terrorists and vigilantes, is also a context in which this threat can be enacted in multiple, similarly "small" and equally disruptive ways.

Notes

1 *Parrhēsia*, Foucault states,

> is a notion which . . . is not integrated in a clearly identifiable and localizable way within a particular conceptual system of philosophical doctrine. It is a theme which runs from one system to another, from one doctrine to another, so that it is quite difficult to define its meaning precisely or identify its precise system.
>
> (2010, 45)

2 In an article I wrote a few years ago, I charged Foucault with focusing on the issues driving Creusa's confessional *parrhēsia* at the expense of the sexual violence that drives her judicial *parrhēsia*. At that time, it seemed to me that Foucault presented the harm Apollo inflicted upon Ion by failing to recognize him as his son as more serious than the sexual violence Apollo inflicted upon Creusa. That charge, in retrospect, doesn't seem quite fair. Foucault makes repeated reference to Creusa being raped (even if the language he uses is somewhat ambiguous – he never actually uses the word rape); moreover, he may emphasize the effects of Ion's appearance on Creusa's life because, at the time, the loss of her social position would have been experienced as the more serious harm (see Taylor 2013).

3 I am referring here to Foucault's essay, "What is Enlightenment?". It is enlightenment, specifically as an ethos or way of life, that he characterizes in this manner (see Foucault 1980c).

4 Brown-Radack does not indicate the exact nature of her assault. She refers to it only as an "incident" (see jucliu 2008a).

5 The surfaces being used were eventually painted black (see jucliu 2008a).

6 One student recounted being told by an administrator after she reported the man whom she had been dating for breaking into her dorm room and raping her that the assault "boiled down to a case of bad chemistry" (Celis 1990).

7 See Butler (2010) on grievability as a marker of a fully livable and therefore injurable life.

8 Girls for Gender Equity, www.ggenyc.org.

9 See Jodi Kantor and Megan Twohey (2017). More than eighty women have made allegations against Weinstein of various forms of sexual violence.

10 https://twitter.com/alyssa_milano/status/919659438700670976?lang=en.

11 Donegan identified herself as the list's creator after learning that Katie Roiphe was going to name her in a forthcoming article for *The Atlantic* (see Donegan 2018).

12 Dixon has also accused L.A. Reid, an executive in the music industry, of sexual harassment. The recent charge of singer R. Kelly with ten counts of sexual abuse is also extremely relevant here (Harris 2019). In a recent *New York Times* op-ed, Lisa VanAllen, who testified against R. Kelly in 2008 and appears in the documentary film, "Surviving R. Kelly," writes that she felt conflicted about testifying against Kelly at that time. On the one hand, she was afraid; not only had she been sexually violated by Kelly, "one of his associates had threatened to kill [her]." On the other hand, in her Chicago neighborhood it was understood that not only did the Black community "[stick] together," but *"Black people [did not] go to the police"* (2019, original emphasis). VanAllen writes that she no longer feels conflicted, and that she spoke out in the documentary in order to "help anyone who has been affected by abuse" (see VanAllen 2019).

13 Lists also appeared on the walls of buildings at Columbia University in 2014 to protest the university's "mishandling of sexual assault allegations" (see Joseph and Swaine 2014).

14 Sclove also filed a Title IX complaint with the U.S. Department of Education (see Kingkade 2014).

15 Karasek discusses, for example, models that take an approach more consistent with restorative justice: "the harm-doer takes responsibility for what happened and a formal plan is developed for the person to make amends and change his behavior" (2018). Jia Tolentino (2018) also discusses alternative ways of addressing and countering campus sexual violence.

16 I include Tarana Burke here although she is now a public figure.

17 The photograph of the woman identified as "hospital worker" shows only part of a side view of her face. The photograph of strawberry picker Isabel Pascual shows her whole face, but her name has been changed "to protect her family." There is no photograph of the woman identified as "former office assistant."

18 Women of color have pointed out that the public faces of #MeToo have largely been white. As Zahara Hill writes, "Black women were quickly isolated from the [#MeToo] dialogue before we could familiarize ourselves with it." Hill notes that when ESPN sports journalist Jemele Hill was suspended and actress and comedian Leslie Jones was harassed by Internet trolls,

> the outrage simply wasn't there for [these] Black women who were put in vulnerable positions by rich White men. White women either have yet to realize or simply choose not to acknowledge there is a common thread between the oppressive powers of the misogyny imposed on [white women in Hollywood] and the white apathy that suppressed Hill's voice.
>
> (2017)

4 Militant bodies

After concluding his 1983 study of political *parrhēsia*, Foucault extended his analysis of the practice of truth-telling by turning his attention the following year to ethical *parrhēsia*. His final course at the Collège de France, *The Courage of Truth*, marks a distinction between the political parrhesiast, who expresses the truth verbally through confronting an unjust individual or institution, and the ethical parrhesiast, who expresses the truth through the totality of the way in which they live their life. Ethical *parrhēsia*, in other words, consists of an embodied ethos that calls into question the prevailing norms and values of society as a whole. Foucault identifies the paradigmatic expression of such an ethos in the mode of existence practiced by the Cynics, whom, he argues, reversed every aspect of a classical way of living that was considered to be the manifestation of the truth. This reversal is not, however, merely oppositional; the Cynic expresses truth, but he does so in and through a critical expression of otherness and difference. Foucault refers to the Cynic way of life as "militant," where militancy entails "bearing witness" to possibilities for new ways of constituting, understanding, and relating to oneself, both generally and in terms of one's relationship to truth; of cultivating and therefore bearing witness to new ways of relating to others and the world; and to cultivating and expressing courage.

My analysis in this chapter parallels my analysis of political *parrhēsia* in Chapter 3. I begin by providing an overview of ethical *parrhēsia* and proceed by way of a more detailed accounting of the ethical *parrhēsia* practiced by the Cynics. I then move into my argument that within a contemporary context, practices bearing the characteristics of militant Cynic ethical *parrhēsia*, like those which emulate judicial *parrhēsia*, possess counter-normalizing/counter-humiliating potential. Especially relevant is the manner in which the Cynic takes on and ultimately turns humiliation back against its source: this subversive embodied manifestation of humiliation undermines the sexual stigmatization that characterizes women's subhumanization. I illustrate the contemporary feminist significance of militant ethical *parrhēsia* through analyzing two forms of anti-sexual violence protest: SlutWalks and Emma Sulkowicz's "Mattress Performance/Carry that Weight" (henceforth MPCW), that reflect some of its defining features. Given that sexual violence is an embodied violation, this analysis elucidates the counter-normalizing/counter-humiliating potential of contemporary manifestations of those features by elucidating these protests' boldly unapologetic, public display and therefore assertion of women's sexually humiliated bodies. This assertion, I show, affords protesters the opportunity to experience their own embodied self-relation differently, in ways that do not produce the normalizing effects of subjectivity upon which sexual humiliation hinges. I conclude by discussing how SlutWalks and MPCW reflect and express a (self)transformative relation to the truth as well as the particular, intensified stakes of ontological risk that characterizes courage when it is practiced not merely through one's speech, but through the totality of how one lives.

I

In his 1983 Collège de France course, Foucault describes how, toward the end of the fifth century, political *parrhēsia* came to occupy a paradoxical position relative to democracy.[1] Political *parrhēsia*'s subsequent decline should not, however, be taken as its demise;[2] nor should it be seen as the demise of *parrhēsia* more generally. Rather, according to Foucault, *parrhēsia* became less a political practice and more a philosophical one. "I think," he explains,

> that there was a sort of gradual diversion of at least a part and a set of functions of *parrhēsia* towards and into philosophical practice which induced . . . a certain inflection of philosophical discourse, philosophical practice, and the philosophical life.
>
> (2010, 341)

Not only philosophy, but also *parrhēsia* and the parrhesiast are changed as a result of these developments. *Parrhēsia* will still be truth-telling, but its ethical character, already inherent in the judicial *parrhēsia* expressed by Creusa, will take prominence such that the parrhesiast will become someone who "holds himself, in a way, aside" from society (Ibid).

Socrates is arguably the most prominent individual practitioner of ethical *parrhēsia*. Socratic *parrhēsia* is ethical because it is concerned with the care of the self and, therefore, with the relation of the self to itself. Foucault describes Socrates as

> someone who is ready to face death rather than renounce truth-telling, but who does not practice this truth-telling by taking the floor in public and saying what he thinks . . . he does so by practicing the testing of souls in the game of ironic cross-examination.
>
> (2011, 73)

Socratic care of the self takes two related yet distinct forms. The first, which Foucault analyzes in 1983 and I discussed in Chapter 1, is elucidated in the *Alcibiades*. Socrates the master guides Alcibiades through the process of properly caring for himself so that he can attain autonomy, govern the city of Athens, and properly care for its citizens (Foucault 2005). Foucault sees reflected in the *Alcibiades* an interconnection of caring for and knowing the self, and hence a concern with the soul, that are characteristic of the Platonic *epistrophē*. In his 1984 analysis of the *Laches*, by contrast, Foucault describes care of the self as taking the form of an ethos, an "aesthetics of existence," or a way of life that is concerned with "how one lives and has lived" (2010, 160). Although this second form of care of the self has, according to Foucault, been neglected within the tradition of Western philosophy, it is not opposed to the more "metaphysical" concern for the soul – nor, Foucault asserts, does he intend to oppose the two. Rather, he identifies within the *Laches* "the moment when the requirement of truth-telling and the principle of the beauty of existence came together in the care of the self" – when, in other words, the classical "true life" becomes concerned with the reality and practicalities of lived experience, with how one creates one's life and conducts oneself (163). To the extent that ethical *parrhēsia* is concerned with how one lives in the world, it is also concerned with caring for the others with whom one shares that world.

In the *Laches*, the interconnection of truth and lived experience finds its expression in the relationship between what one says and what one does. From Foucault's perspective, when Laches agrees to enter into dialogue with Socrates, his is not seeking merely to gain "technical knowledge" (2011, 146). Socrates will therefore direct Laches in a different manner than he did Alcibiades. Through acting as a "touchstone," subjecting him to testing that enables him to "distinguish between the good and bad [he] has done in life," Socrates will provide Laches with insight into his own mode of living (145). Through constructing an "account of himself," Laches will gain experience in and therefore learn how to properly care for himself; this experience will position him to assist others in doing the same (144). Socrates is qualified to provide this sort of instruction because what he says, his verbal instruction, is in "harmony" with how "he lives" (148). Ethical *parrhēsia* is thus not a means of gaining knowledge about the nature of truth. It is a way of practicing or manifesting the truth through one's overall mode of existence: one's relationship to oneself, and to others, and to the world more broadly.

The most important expression of ethical *parrhēsia* for Foucault occurs not in the individual life of Socrates, but rather in the collective mode of existence practiced by the Cynics. "Cynicism," Foucault states, "appears ... to be a form of philosophy in which mode of life and truth-telling are directly and immediately linked to each other" (2011, 166). Despite some broad similarities with its Socratic counterpart, the Cynic mode of existence is "distinctive . . . with very characteristic, well-defined rules, conditions,

[and] modes" (165). First, and consistent with the idea that practicing ethical *parrhēsia* sets one apart from the rest of society, Socrates' way of living conflicted with prevailing norms and values of Greek society. At the same time, Socrates never wavered in his loyalty to Athens. The Cynic, in contrast, did not belong to and was therefore not bound by any particular society. His role is to "run ahead of humanity," acting as a kind of "scout" who seeks out and determines in advance what is "favorable or hostile to man" and then returns to convey what he has discovered (167). This nomadic existence further removes the Cynics from society: inability to earn a living, maintain a permanent dwelling place, or accumulate possessions positions them on the fringes as "beggars." Dirty, dressed in rags, and carrying a staff, the Cynic is the embodiment of his mode of existence. "Cynic poverty," Foucault states, "is . . . a real, material, and physical poverty" (257). Second, while mode of existence and truth-telling are interconnected within the lives and practices of both Socrates and the Cynics, Foucault argues that the latter forge this connection "in a much tighter, more precise way," insofar as they see the defining characteristics of their mode of life as "condition[s] for the possibility of truth-telling" (172). If the Cynic had possessions, attachments, and relationships, he would be preoccupied with them and therefore unable to attend to the needs of humanity as a whole. The "reductive" nature of Cynic poverty, moreover, strips away "pointless" social convention that simultaneously masks and detracts from the truth, thereby revealing life as it "ought to be." In sum, within the context of the Cynic life, one manifests the truth in "one's acts, one's body, the way one dresses, and in the way one conducts oneself and lives" (Ibid).

The possibility of truth becoming manifest through the kind of life lived by the Cynics as opposed to the life of Socrates, according to Foucault, confronts, challenges, and inverts the traditional ancient Greek notion of the true life (*bios alēthēs*). The defining principles of the true life correspond to four prevailing definitions of the word "truth" (*alethes, aletheia*). The first principle, that the true life "hides nothing of its intentions and aims," that it is a life of "non-concealment," corresponds to the definition of truth as that which is neither "hidden" nor "concealed" (Foucault 2011, 221–225; 253; 218–219). Second, within the context of the true life, "good is not mixed with evil, pleasure with suffering, [nor] virtue with vice" (221–225). This second principle, Foucault notes, was construed in two different ways: as an "aesthetics of purity" and as an aesthetics of "independence" and "self-sufficiency" (255–256). It corresponds to the definition of truth as that which is "unalloyed" – not mixed with and therefore not obscured by anything else. Third, the true life is "in line with the principles, the rules, the nomos" (221–225). That is, the true life conforms to both laws of nature and societal norms and conventions. This principle corresponds to the definition of truth as "that which is straight," devoid of misleading "twists and turns." Finally, the idea that the true life is sovereign in the sense that it "shuns disturbance, change, [and] corruption" is consistent with the definition of truth as that which is "unchangeable and incorruptible." Taken as a whole, the true life was considered to be "divine," "blessed," and happy (218–219; 221–225; 265).

The Cynic life is a subversive reflection – a "grimace" – of the true life (Foucault 2011, 227). This subversion proceeds, Foucault shows, by means of a process the Cynics referred to as "changing the value of the currency." Pointing to etymological resonances between the Greek words *nomisma* (currency) and *nomos* (law), Foucault explains that, in broad terms, "[t]o change the value of the currency is . . . to adopt a certain standpoint towards convention, rule, or law" (Ibid). The Cynics do not dispense with the true life – they do not *de*value the coin. Rather, the Cynic mode of existence "scandalous[ly] revers[es]" the true life as convention, rule, and law – both generally as a norm and more specifically as an ideal. This scandalous reversal entails pushing each of the true life's defining principles to its limit; revealing those limits in turn forces the principle into a confrontation with itself that changes its meaning. The true life's value is "restored" through its being "stamped" with a different effigy – through, in other words, its own subversion (Ibid). This new, Cynic, effigy is the life of a dog.

The Cynic dog's life, Foucault shows, is characterized by shamelessness, indifference, discrimination, and aggressive service/protection, principles that constitute limit manifestations of the true life's four defining principles. First, the Cynic performs publicly that which "only dogs and animals dare to do and which men usually hide" (Foucault 2011, 243). Boldly and publicly performing acts normed as private is the limit manifestation of the lack of concealment that characterizes the true life. Second, Cynic life is "indifferent." The Cynic "has no needs other than those [he] can satisfy immediately;" he does not require human attachments, possessions, or relationships (Ibid). Foucault recounts that Diogenes, for example, wore very little clothing and lived and died in the street. This "ugly, dirty, dependent, and humiliated" Cynic life of poverty constitutes the limit manifestation of the true life's "unalloyed independence;" it is a willfully abject life that neither generates pity nor requests assistance (259). Third, the Cynic possesses heightened awareness of, and is therefore able to make, important distinctions: "the good from the bad, the true from the false, and masters from enemies." His is a "life of discernment which knows how to prove, test, and distinguish." The Cynic's acumen makes him, more specifically, a "guard dog" whose life is dedicated to serving and protecting others. Foucault relates that the Cynic life is "a life which barks." The loud, assertive discernment practiced by the Cynics is the limit manifestation of the true life's adherence to the law (263–265).

Foucault does not overtly carry the dog's life metaphor into his discussion of Cynic subversion of sovereignty, the true life's fourth and definitive principle. Still, it is apparent from his analysis that the metaphor applies. Within the context of the true life, sovereignty refers to a mode of self-relation characterized by "enjoyment," understood in terms of both "possession and pleasure" (Foucault 2011, 270). A sovereign life is one that is "in possession of itself, a life of which no fragment, no element escapes the exercise of its power . . . over itself. Being sovereign is first and foremost being one's own, belonging to oneself" (271). The sovereign life also "takes pleasure in [it]self;" in, that is, its own self-ownership (Ibid). Cultivating a self-relation of sovereignty also affects one's external relationships: sovereign individuals are able to properly care for others (as seen in certain relationships such as those between pupil and teacher, or between friends) and they therefore serve as exemplars (272–273). Foucault emphasizes that within the context of the true life, the self-relation is interconnected with relations to others: "[t]he same founding act of taking possession of self by self gives me enjoyment of myself . . . and enables me to be useful to others in their trouble or misfortune" (273).

The limit manifestation of the true life's sovereignty is, Foucault contends, a sort of monarchy. The Cynic, precisely in his impoverishment, is exalted as a king. Like sovereignty, Cynic monarchy is characterized by an interconnection of self-to-self and self-to-other relations. In keeping with the guard dog principle, these relations take the form of "battles." Rather than uncritically affirming his current self-relation, however, the Cynic wages war on his "internal enemies" (his "appetites" and vices) through "relentless work on [him]self" that "[pushes] back the limits of what he can bear" (Foucault 2011, 279). Engaging in self-combat also provides training for attacking, more broadly, humanity's vices, including and especially its uncritical acceptance of conventions and conventionality. In sum, the Cynic is an "aggressive benefactor" who "battles both for [and against] himself and for [and against] others" (280; 283). Foucault describes the Cynic as an "anti-king king" who reveals the "hollow, illusory, and precarious" nature of prevailing modes of thought and existence (275).

Foucault characterizes the Cynic's radically oppositional pushing to their limits, subversion, and transformation of the defining principles of the true life as "militant." Cynic militancy does not express a will to domination. Rather, it is the specifically paradigmatic expression of the Cynic scandalous reversal of the true life. Militant Cynic ethical *parrhēsia* entails a mode of existence that "bear[s] witness," and which does so through "break[ing] with the conventions, habits, and values of society" (Foucault 2011, 184). It simultaneously expresses prevailing modes of existence and their subversion in a way that exposes convention in its conventionality, habit in its thoughtless reproduction. Notably, within a contemporary context, a mode of existence so characterized would express prevailing norms in ways that expose them in their normalization. Through bearing witness, a militant mode of existence ultimately opens onto the possibility of alternatives.

Militancy bears witness, first, to alternative modes of self-relation. A sovereign self-relation is static; it uncritically affirms itself in its own state of self-mastery. In Cynic *parrhēsia*, by contrast, the self-relation claims ownership of itself through becoming other not only with respect to prevailing social norms and practices but also with respect to itself. The non-attachment that characterizes the Cynic self-relation can be seen as the limit manifestation of loosening self-attachments, of a self-relation that is always and at the same time a self-transformation; it embodies the risk Judith Butler identifies in becoming "questionable in one's ontology" (2004, 191). In taking that risk, Cynic militancy bears witness to the "possibility and evident value of an *other* life" (Foucault 2011, 184). Through living a life that is not merely unconventional but in fact lays bare and confronts convention in and as conventionality, Cynic militancy aims to and in fact does "change the world" (285). The Cynic way of life is militant in part because it bears witness to the possibility of, as Foucault puts it elsewhere, "thinking differently than one thinks and perceiving differently than one sees," as well as to ways in which the transformative effects of thinking and perceiving differently extend beyond the individual (Foucault 1990b, 9).

The second way in which militancy bears witness is thus apparent in the fact that, given their interconnection, alternative modes of self-relation facilitate alternative modes of relating to others and world: "[a]n *other* life for an *other* world" (Foucault 2011, 287). This "other world," Foucault makes clear, is neither a Platonic realm of Ideas nor a Christian afterlife that transcends lived experience. Rather, the "other world" that different modes of self-relation and other/world relations create is a transformation within and of the current world: for the Cynics, "a true life . . . is an other life in *this* world" (319; my emphasis).

Third, Cynic militancy bears witness to alternative ways of conceptualizing and relating to the notion of truth – and therefore to constituting oneself in terms of it. According to Foucault, the truth is made manifest in and through the militant otherness of the Cynic way of life. To be sure, it may well not be a manifestation that is readily recognizable, given that it "breaks totally and on every point with . . . traditional forms of existence" (244). The crucial point here for Foucault is the fact that through their mode of existence the Cynics embody and thereby illustrate the possibility of truth becoming manifest not through adherence to convention – not, in other words, through obedience to prevailing modes of thought and existence. Otherness and difference, not sameness, become both a condition for the possibility and a characteristic of truth. As the grimace of the true life, the "broken mirror in which philosophy is at once called upon to see itself and fails to recognize itself," Foucault argues, the Cynics' mode of existence "[fulfills] the true life" precisely "as a demand for a life" and a world which are "radically other" (270).

Finally, militancy bears witness to the parrhesiast's courage. As Foucault describes it, Cynic ethical *parrhēsia* is all-encompassing. The Cynic challenges "people to condemn, reject, despise, and insult the very manifestations of what they accept, or claim to accept at the level of principles;" the Cynic also "fac[es] up to [the] anger" of those he challenges (Foucault 2011,

234). Given the scope and intensity of its critique, practicing Cynic ethical *parrhēsia* requires courage. "In the case of the Cynic scandal," Foucault asserts,

> one risks one's life, not just by telling the truth, and in order to tell it, but by the very way in which one lives. In all the meanings of the word, one "exposes" one's life. That is to say . . . [o]ne risks it by displaying it; and it is because one displays it that one risks it. One exposes one's life, not through one's discourses, but through one's life itself.
>
> (Ibid)

Given Foucault's account of the nature and function of normalizing power, as well as his identification of the self-relation as a fundamental site for both its (re)production and countering, his interest in militant Cynic ethical *parrhēsia* seems clear. Within a contemporary context, practices possessing militant characteristics would express normative frames of recognition in ways that bring them into an aggressive confrontation with themselves, confrontation that at least generates conditions for the possibility of their "breaking with themselves," if not that breakage itself (Butler 2010, 24). The provocation of militantly counter-normalizing practices and modes of self-relation and other/world relations is, moreover, both insistent and persistent; it cannot, therefore, be easily or comfortably ignored or dismissed. Revealing the limits of prevailing norms in ways that inhibit their seamless reproduction, militancy bears witness to both normalization and the possibility of its undermining – the possibility of difference, something other than what currently exists, alternatives. Exercising this sort of ongoing incitement of difference relative to one's relation to oneself overtly and directly counters the self-renunciation, obedience, and conformity (and inculcation of the same) that define subjectivity as a normalizing mode of self-relation.

Foucault's analysis also, and more specifically, points to the counter-humiliating character of militant Cynic ethical *parrhēsia*. This subversion occurs by way of the Cynic dog's life "scandalous reversal" of the true life. Referring to themselves as dogs reflects the Cynics' internalization of "respectable" society's perception of them as subhuman, less than fully livable lives and their resulting treatment as if nonhuman. That the Cynics do not, however, (re)constitute themselves in terms of subhumanization and humiliation in the sense of acquiescing to and therefore merely reproducing them is apparent in two ways. First, the Cynics used the experience of humiliation (which included not only verbal but also physical abuse) as an "exercise" or training in cultivating indifference, construed in terms of both "physical endurance" and a dispassionate attitude toward others' opinions (Foucault 2011, 299). Indifference, as discussed earlier, subverts the unmitigated independence of the true life. While experiencing humiliation affords the Cynic the opportunity to engage in battle with and thereby strengthen himself through self-testing, what the Cynic actually bolsters are his own critical and creative capacities.

Self-testing functions as a mode of self-critique and self-challenging that exposes and brings him into confrontation with his current limits in ways that facilitate self-transformation. The Cynic, in other words, asserts himself through becoming other to himself. As Foucault shows, a clear distinction can therefore be drawn between Cynic humiliation as a form of oppositionally transformative self-testing and early Christian asceticism that is both grounded in and reproduces a self-relation characterized by self-renunciation, obedience, and conformity (317–321).[3] In contrast to the early Christian self-relation in which any assertion of self is simultaneously a renunciation of self, within the militant Cynic way of life, there is no assertion of self that is not simultaneously a critique and transformation of self.

Second, given the interconnection of the self-relation with relations to others and world, when the Cynic tests, subverts, and transforms himself by way of the experience of humiliation, he is likewise subjecting to critique broader, conventional norms of "honor and dishonor." His public, embodied expression of humiliation pushes those norms to their limits, confronts them with themselves, disrupts their uncritical reproduction, and thus opens onto other possibilities. Foucault describes, for example, an occasion upon which Diogenes was eating in public and summarily ridiculed for behaving like a dog. Diogenes' response was to assert that only other dogs would surround a dog who possessed food (Foucault 2011, 262). Foucault identifies in Diogenes' response not acquiescence but subversion of the true life's characteristic of non-concealment. Diogenes turns the humiliation that is inflicted upon him back onto itself and confronts it with itself; through that confrontation, conventional notions of humiliation and dishonor become other to themselves and are reversed.

As I have already implied, like his analysis of political *parrhēsia*, Foucault's analysis of the Cynic way of life should not be construed as suggesting that ethical *parrhēsia* can be revived within a contemporary context. Rather, in pointing to the counter-normalizing/counter-humiliating potential of contemporary modes of existence – practices, self-relation, and other/world relations – that reflect the oppositionally transformative character of militant Cynic ethical *parrhēsia*, Foucault shows that the work of counter-normalization can be undertaken broadly, though one's overall way of life. Even as he reiterates it, then, he also expands the three-fold task of which that work consists: (1) critically engaging our own present in order to identify contemporary practices that reflect and may therefore promote at least aspects of the kind of counter-normalizing self-relation reflected in militant Cynic ethical *parrhēsia*; (2) critically analyzing those practices in order to more fully understand the conditions from which they emerge; and (3) fostering conditions under which a plurality of counter-normalizing modes of existence may proliferate.

As I did in Chapter 3, I proceed here by taking up this three-fold task. The next section of the chapter analyzes two feminist anti-sexual violence protests, SlutWalks and MPCW, the ontologically risky character of which reflects counter-normalization and counter-humiliation, and generates counter-normalizing/counter-humiliating effects.[4] Like the ontologically risky speech of victims/survivors in the Holtzclaw case, the Brown University victims/survivors, and the women of #MeToo, SlutWalks and MPCW (re)direct humiliation outward by means of public confrontation. Within the context of these protests, such confrontation manifests in ways that reflect defining aspects of Cynic shamelessness: SlutWalks and MPCW simultaneously assert and subvert norms surrounding what can be expressed publicly and what is normed as private and therefore internalized; this expression and subversion, moreover, are embodied.[5] In addition, MPCW reflects significant aspects of Cynic indifference: the protest simultaneously expresses and subverts the self-containment, self-referentiality, and self-mastery that characterize modern Western subjectivity and, again, this expression and subversion is generated in and through the body. As with ethical *parrhēsia* more generally, SlutWalks and MPCW confront not merely an individual or institution, but also prevailing norms and, therefore, relations of power.

Unlike militant Cynic ethical *parrhēsia*, in SlutWalks and MPCW this confrontation does not scandalously *reverse* prevailing norms or, therefore, eradicate normalization; nor, therefore, do the protests reverse and eradicate sexual humiliation. Rather, SlutWalks and MPCW scandalously, critically, and aggressively *confront and thus engage* normalization: they disrupt the reproduction of prevailing gendered power relations that generate sexual violence and sexual humiliation. Subversion of the sexual(ized) stigma that defines and reinforces women's subhumanization is a key mechanism of this disruption. The protests deploy in oppositionally transformative ways cultural markers of the inferiority of women's sexed and sexualized bodies and, therefore, of their subhumanity. That is to say, SlutWalks and MPCW subversively express, expose, unsettle, and thus open onto resignification of the normalizing reduction of sexually vulnerable and sexually violated bodies to that vulnerability and violation. In doing so, the protests bear witness to possibilities for modes of self-relation that deviate from and facilitate the countering of characteristics of subjectivity that reinforce sexual humiliation. Experiencing alternative modes of their own embodied self-relation on the part of protesters opens onto new modes of relating to others and the world; the protests thus also bear witness to the courage of protesters who endeavor to constitute, understand, and relate to themselves differently. At the heart of the protests is the oppositional Cynic attitude of "basically" saying "what everyone says and yet mak[ing] the very fact of saying it unacceptable" (Foucault 2011, 233).

II

The first SlutWalk, which took place in Toronto in April of 2011, was organized by York University students Heather Jarvis, Sonya Barnett, Alyssa Teekah, Jeanette Janzen, and Erika Jane Scholz (Millar 2011). The protest, which called attention to and criticized the practice of victim-blaming in instances of sexual violence, was held in response to a remark made by

Toronto Police Constable Michael Sanguinetti during a sexual assault prevention program held at York that January. To avoid being sexually assaulted
and raped, Sanguinetti asserted, women should refrain from "dressing like
sluts" (Stampler 2011). Three thousand people participated in the Toronto
protest that in turn inspired SlutWalks around the world (Contreras 2011).

SlutWalks have drawn feminist criticism for a variety of reasons. Some
critics see the protests endeavoring to reclaim the notion of sluttiness, and
simply and fundamentally disagree with such an objective. Gail Dines and
Wendy Murphy argue that 'the term "slut" is so deeply rooted in the patriarchal . . . view of women's sexuality that it is beyond redemption . . . trying
to change its meaning is a waste of precious feminist resources' (2011). The
fact that many protesters wear sexually provocative clothing has generated
controversy as well. Some see the short skirts, low-cut tops, and lingerie
worn by many SlutWalk protesters reproducing the same sexist constructions of women's sexuality that ground and are reproduced by the normalizing gendered relations of power that, in turn, ground and reproduce
conditions for the possibility of sexual violence. Still other feminist critics
charge that the provocative dress, and the attention it draws, undermines
the protests' point that women's clothing is unrelated to the perpetration
of sexual violence. "[W]hile the mission of SlutWalks is crucial," writes
Rebecca Traister, "the package is confusing and leaves young feminists
open to the very kinds of attacks they are battling" (2011).

Black women have argued that SlutWalk organizers and participants fail
to acknowledge the white privilege reflected in the term "slut," its negative
connotations notwithstanding. Given the construction of Black women's
sexuality in terms of ready sexual availability, the Black women authors
of an open letter to SlutWalk organizers assert, they cannot be viewed as
having fallen from a state purity, a descent that the concept "slut" implies.
"Although we vehemently support a woman's right to wear whatever
she wants anytime, anywhere," write the open letter's authors, 'as Black
women, we do not have the privilege or the space to call ourselves "slut"
without validating the already, historically entrenched ideology and recurring messages about what and who the Black woman is.'[6] By way of
countering the protests' predominantly white and otherwise privileged
character, activist Amber Rose has been organizing a SlutWalk in Los
Angeles since 2015.[7] Rose's protest, which emphasizes sex-positivity and
inclusivity, has attracted increasing numbers of participants each year.
Consistent with intersectional feminist activism, Rose has intentionally
and effectively reached out to both women of color and the LGBTQ community. "The crowd and the lineup of performers and presenters," Kristen
Sollee writes, "reflected [Rose's] effort, and so Black Lives Matter signs
were front and center, as were those that challenged the gender binary and
the idea that feminism is for cisgender women alone" (2017). SlutWalk Los
Angeles, Rose asserts, welcomes the LGBTQ community: "Whatever gender you identify with you are accepted with open arms" (Gore 2018). She

has also sought to expand the protest not merely in terms of the diversity of its participants, but in terms of its areas of focus. The 2018 event, for example, endeavored to increase women's political engagement, in part by including voter registration.

Especially in light of Rose's intersectional activism, I don't think, despite their mixed reception and shortcomings, that SlutWalks should be dismissed out of hand. On my reading, not only do the protests resist being reduced to an effort to reclaim the term "slut," they also reflect a "scandalous" – not, as I have emphasized, "reversal" – but rather disruptive confrontation with conditions for the possibility as well as the experience of sexual humiliation.[8] Embodiment generally and embodied exposure more specifically are key mechanisms of this confrontation. As discussed in Chapter 2, sexual humiliation hinges on internalized exposure and display. Victims' embodied (sexual) capacities are appropriated by perpetrators in ways that reduce those capacities to mechanisms of subhumanization and, therefore, subjugation: the sexually humiliated body reproduces prevailing norms and, hence, gendered relations of power that facilitate and legitimize sexual violence. Humiliated victims/survivors experience their bodies as material manifestations of their own sexual degradation; they therefore seek to deflect attention and/or detach from them.

SlutWalks subvert the internalization and sexualized stigmatization that underpin and are reasserted by means of sexual violence and sexual humiliation. The public exposure and display of both the body itself and particular modes of dress (both of which function as loci of stigma) function as a limit-expression of stigmatizing, sexist constructions of women's sexuality. Display of their breasts, a part of the body that marks women as men's inferior others within the context of gendered power relations, by topless SlutWalk protesters is subversive. At the same time that men spectators may ogle, the context of the protest, as well as marks on the body – anti-rape slogans such as "A kiss is not a contract;" "Don't tell me how to dress, tell them not to rape;" "Still not asking for it" – make clear that not only are these bodies not for men, they oppose men's sexist, normalizing gaze. Protesters' embodied exposure breaks with convention; in doing so, it brings into confrontation with itself the gendered norming of women's bodies as being only for men, as well as the gendered terms under which men are considered the legitimate determiners of when, how, where, and for whom women's bodies may be displayed. Sexually provocative dress, especially that which, like lingerie, is largely normed as being for men's consumption, functions in a similarly oppositional, transformative way. Its seemingly contradictory appearance within the context of an anti-sexual violence protest pushes to their limit and exposes normalizing norms that reduce women merely to sexed, sexualized, and therefore inferior sub-humans.[9] While, as I note, SlutWalks have generated normalizing sexist responses, they have also generated ridicule, appreciation, dismissal, and critical reflection. Whether positive or negative, the existence of a diversity of responses to the protests reflects a deviation from the mere sexualization of scantily or partially clad women's bodies and, hence, the potential of the protests to disrupt uncritical reproduction of normalizing norms and the representations they (re)produce.

What is perhaps the most disruptive form of exposure and display in Slut-Walks occurs through public avowal not only of women's bodies that are normed as sexually vulnerable and therefore potentially violable, but of sexually violated bodies. For SlutWalk participants who are victims/survivors of sexual violence, embodied exposure – sexually explicit or not – acquires increased significance and meaning. Such exposure entails refusal of and therefore overtly oppositional confrontation with stigmatizing gendered constructions of sexually humiliated bodies as needing to be concealed. Protesters who march in the clothes they were wearing when they were raped or sexually assaulted – everything from "pajamas to thigh-high boots" to "green and gold" sequins – publicly display and thus assert rather than renounce or disavow an embodied self-relation upon which sexual violence has been inflicted, not despite but rather precisely in its susceptibility to violation (Tillet 2011). As my account of the dynamics of sexual humiliation shows, not only sexual violence itself but also victims'/survivors' responses to it are "scripted."[10] Both entail "a series of steps and signals" that are generated by and reassert gendered relations of power (Marcus 1992, 390). To the extent that sexual humiliation is a scripted response to sexual violence, refusing one of its defining steps – the internalization upon which it hinges – disrupts its uncritical reproduction; this refusal enables script "revision," or even abandonment (391). Through publicly and corporeally expressing both precariousness and its exploitation, the protesters in question gain a different, counter-stigmatizing (and therefore counter-humiliating), potentially empowering experience of their own embodied self-relation.

Like the SlutWalk protests, Emma Sulkowicz's MPCW subverts the internalization and sexualized stigmatization that characterize sexual humiliation.[11] At the beginning of her sophomore year as a student at Columbia, Sulkowicz filed a complaint with the university in which she stated that she had been raped in her dorm room by a fellow student, Paul Nungesser. The following year, 2013, Columbia found Nungesser "not to be responsible" (Smith 2014). Sulkowicz responded to this outcome by creating MPCW, an endurance performance art piece that served as both her senior project and a political protest. For as long as Nungesser remained enrolled at Columbia during the 2014–2015 academic year, Sulkowicz determined that she would carry with her at all times while on campus a mattress like the one upon which she had been assaulted (Ibid).[12] The performance/protest was intended to illustrate the burden victims/survivors of sexual violence experience, especially when they know their attackers have walked free.[13]

As is the case with SlutWalk participants who are themselves victims/survivors, Sulkowicz publicly asserts, rather than masks or disavows, the openness and exposure and hence potential for violation that stem from the interconnection of the self-relation with relations to others and world. Through publicly displaying her own sexually violated and humiliated body, she counters its stigmatization; by redirecting that violation and humiliation outward, toward its source, she counters internalization. Whereas in SlutWalks mode of dress functions in a counter-stigmatizing manner, MPCW counters stigmatization through its endurance aspect and, hence, through the mattress itself. Carrying and thus publicly displaying the fifty-pound object within the space of Columbia's campus for an entire year materially expresses the burden that sexual violation and humiliation inflicts upon victims. Sulkowicz's protest can thus be seen as a form of self-testing akin to that practiced by the Cynics in the face of humiliation. Sulkowicz takes on this burden – she carries the mattress – and one of the "rules of engagement" for MPCW was that she could not ask others to help her carry it. At the same time, Sulkowicz does not merely *accept* this burden, and counter-stigmatization is apparent in her critical deployment of it. It is not only the mattress and thus the site of violation that is displayed in MPCW, it is also the sexually violated body that carries it. Lugging around not merely fifty pounds, but an awkwardly shaped and difficult to maneuver fifty-pound object, for an entire academic year made Sulkowicz physically stronger. MPCW thus transformed her body and her own experience of it in ways that undermine the reductive construction of women's embodied self-relation to a merely inferior, merely sexualized, other; (self)transformation occurred through taking on of the burden of sexual humiliation in an oppositional and therefore disruptive way.

The rule that Sulkowicz cannot request help in carrying the mattress could be taken as a reflection and reassertion of the self-containment, self-referentiality, and self-legitimation that characterize subjectivity as a mode of self-relation. What might appear as a (self)masterful assertion of self in MPCW is undermined, however, by a second rule of engagement: Sulkowicz can accept help *if it is offered*. It is at the intersection of these two rules that the Cynic-like indifference of MPCW emerges: self-assertion occurs, but it does so in and through asserting relation to others. An indifferent self-relation is thus characterized by acknowledgment of and engagement with the reality that living in a shared world exposes one to "impinging and being impinged upon by" others in ways one can neither anticipate nor control (Butler 2010). Under these conditions, assertion of self entails the transformation of self. Sulkowicz sets the terms for MPCW, but she cannot know the effects of either accepting or refusing aid: acceptance might lead to an interaction in which she is able to meaningfully convey her experience of being raped, or which ends up reinforcing conditions for the possibility of sexual humiliation; individuals whose help is refused might try to insist, experience hurt feelings, or respond with anger or overt hostility.

Potential helpers are thus also transformed through an assertion of themselves that entails their own exposure. Whether their offer of assistance is accepted or not, in extending themselves beyond themselves, they risk their own self-attachment, and in doing so are confronted with their own expo-sure by way of an uncertain encounter through which they will be changed. Helpers' awareness of or existing commitment to working to combat sexual violence may be raised or increased. Those whose offers of help are refused may be inspired to engage in critical self-reflection concerning why and thus undergo a shift in how they perceive themselves; conversely, they may go away feeling that their worst views of feminism have been confirmed. It's also possible that, whether or not their offer of aid is accepted, some people will be changed simply through becoming aware of the mutual interdepend-ency of their own existence with that of another. Whatever transpires, a self-relation characterized by indifference recognizes and engages its inter-connection with relations to others and world. Offering to help Sulkowicz, writes Rebecca Mead, is "not just a gesture of simple human empathy" (2015). Such offers, rather, became "a means of protesting sexual violence and expressing solidarity with those who have experienced it" (Ibid).[14]

Through their contemporary enactments of shamelessness, and indiffer-ence, SlutWalks and MPCW counter sexual stigmatization through disrupt-ing the reproduction of norms of display and exposure and, therefore, the internalization sexual humiliation both demands and intensifies. By exter-nalizing these norms, the protests expose and challenge their limits and in doing so bring them into confrontation with themselves such that alternatives become possible. Given that the uncritical reproduction of sexual humilia-tion is bound up with subjectivity as a mode of self-relation, Sulkowicz and SlutWalk participants can be seen to have an experience of constituting, un-derstanding, and relating to themselves not merely or simply as subjects and, therefore, in ways that disrupt the normalizing cycle of self-assertion and self-renunciation which keeps sexual violation constitutive of who victims/ survivors are. Insofar as subjectivity is equally bound up with intelligibility, such alternative modes of self-relation may appear merely contradictory or even nonsensical; taking them up therefore risks the suspension of the in-telligibility of those who do so. Yet it is within this risk, as Foucault makes clear with respect to both political and ethical *parrhēsia*, that possibilities for difference and hence for counter-normalization and counter-humiliation emerge. Taking this risk both recognizes the possibility of and experiments with constituting oneself "beyond the norms of recognition, even as [one] makes a new demand for recognition;" it thus confronts the question of "how to live and thrive at the borders of recognizability" (Butler 2004, 193).

As my analysis of disinterestedness illustrates, given the interconnection of the relation of self to self with the relation of self to others, relating to oneself differently both facilitates and extends into self-other relations. MPCW, as noted above, affords the opportunity for others to actually 'en-ter into "the space of performance"' and to be transformed through that experience (Edwards 2014). 'By quite literally bringing the site of the crime (in this case an ostensibly "safe" domestic space) into public sight,' Stassa Edwards writes, "Sulkowicz's performance relocates its subject in between the shifting grounds of public and private, personal and political" (Ibid).

SlutWalks likewise have the potential, especially for victims/survivors, to generate or deepen acknowledgment of and engagement with the self-relation's interconnection with relations to others and world in ways that foster new modes of self-other relations among participants. New modes of relating might also emerge between participants and spectators, with the latter, as in MPCW, being brought into the space of protest; in this way, relations between spectators could thus be transformed as well.

Consistent with my illustration of the ongoing, partial, and potentially fraught character of counter-normalization and counter-humiliation, I have shown that, like the other forms of feminist anti-sexual violence protest I have analyzed, SlutWalks and MPCW counter but do not eradicate normalization and sexual humiliation; moreover, they themselves possess normalizing potential. Still, the difference and (self)transformation the protests generate themselves facilitate navigation of existing power relations in ways that open onto (potentially a proliferation of) "other," potentially counter-normalizing alternatives. The disruption of prevailing norms and normalizing relations of power generated by experiencing non-normative modes of constituting, understanding, and relating to oneself, and therefore to others and the world, "breaks with the conventions, habits, and values of society," producing the kind of slippage between norms and their reproduction Butler describes. When victims/survivors risk their intelligibility and in doing so counter both sexual humiliation and the conditions for its uncritical reproduction, they "refuse to be dishonored by dishonor," and that refusal, in turn, bears witness to possibilities for alternative modes of existence – for a collective "other life" aimed at producing social change. As I shall argue in the book's conclusion, the militancy of these protests extends, or at least has the potential to extend, beyond the context of the protests themselves.

Like the practices I considered in Chapter 3, SlutWalks and MPCW also express truths about sexual violence against women. And like the militant ethical *parrhēsia* of the Cynics, the protests do so by challenging and subverting prevailing modes of thought and existence such that truth becomes manifest through difference and otherness that is expressed materially in acts, the body, dress, and way of life. For the Cynic, truth is conveyed through an embodied expression of otherness that occurs by way of critique and transformation of self-relation and other/world relations. I have shown that in SlutWalks and MPCW, it is protesters' embodied expressions that simultaneously convey and subvert prevailing norms governing women's gendered, sexualized otherness, as well as their sexuality. The protests expose in their normalization gendered relations of power within the context of which women's sexually violable and violated bodies are seen to convey only the truth of women's subhumanity and, therefore, the legitimacy of their treatment as if nonhuman.

SlutWalks and MPCW, in other words, bodily confront normalizing truth in its normalization. Like those of the Cynics, protesters' bodies reflect the "thoughtless conventionality" of normative ways of understanding and responding to sexual violence back onto and against society in ways that disrupt their uncritical reproduction and through doing so facilitate the assertion of victims'/survivors' oppositional, subjugated, uncomfortable truths about sexual violence. This mirroring, disruption, and assertion expresses the "doubling effect" that, as discussed in Chapter 3, characterizes political *parrhēsia*, whereby truth becomes manifest in both the stance of the self-relation, and the effects generated by that stance. In SlutWalks and MPCW, protesters assert, take ownership of, and bind themselves to themselves through becoming other than what they currently are. The simultaneous binding of themselves to the truth that occurs in the doubling thus conveys truth not through validating what already exists but rather, as is the case with the Cynics, through difference and the possibility onto which it opens. Asserting and affirming the sexed and sexualized body in ways that turns its reduction to mere susceptibility to openness and exposure and, hence, to violation, back upon and therefore exposes the source of that reduction disrupts reconstitution of the self-relation in terms of subhumanity. Refusing and exposing as oppressive the role of "loyal vassal," protesters act not as mirrors in which men are able to see themselves reflected as superior, fully livable lives (Bergoffen 2017). Rather, like the Cynic, these protesting women assert themselves as broken mirrors that call upon a sexist, misogynist society to see, to recognize, and to reckon with itself. SlutWalk and MPCW simultaneously reflect and open onto the redirection of critical and creative capacities outward, toward self- and broader transformation. In my view, then, the protests' militancy extends beyond their boundaries. For participants, just as for the Cynics, militancy manifests in terms of actions, embodiment, clothing – all of which, as Foucault makes clear, are elements of how "one conducts oneself and lives" within the context of everyday life (Foucault 2011).

III

By way of concluding, I want to discuss how the SlutWalk and MPCW protests bear witness not only to possibilities for counter-normalizing/counter-humiliating (self)transformation, but also to protesters' courage. Political *parrhēsia*, Foucault shows, requires courage because the parrhesiast who practices it puts their life at risk. In *The Courage of Truth*, he shows that militant Cynic ethical *parrhēsia* entails the same risk. While the particular dynamics of judicial *parrhēsia* in particular (i.e., a disempowered individual publicly confronting a powerful one concerning an injustice the latter has committed against them) may seem to position the political parrhesiast as taking on greater and more direct risk and, hence, as more courageous than their ethical counterpart, on my reading, Foucault is not drawing such a contrast between the two forms of truth-telling. Even if he is, it is not that difference that interests me here. As I see it, at stake is not so much *the degree of the risk itself* that one faces in practicing one form or the other of *parrhēsia*, but rather *the extent to which one takes on risk – the scope and depth of the risk*. The political parrhesiast risks their life, and thus exhibits courage, when they speak out against individual and institutional injustices; the ethical parrhesiast risks their life by living – their embodied mode of existence is an affront to oppressive conventionality and its uncritical acceptance in all of its myriad forms. In ethical *parrhēsia*, then, courage is bound up with simply being alive. Both political and ethical *parrhēsia* reveal and challenge oppression that has gone unchallenged and for that reason political and ethical parrhesiasts alike are seen as threats. Political parrhesiasts, while they pose a direct and immediate threat to particular and overt normalizing practices, are not constantly or persistently threatening. The threat of ethical *parrhēsia*, while more diffuse, is also more pervasive, in terms of the relation of self to self, the relation of self to other/world, and the social critique it generates. Equally threatening, therefore, are contemporary ontologically risky practices that reveal and counter normalization in these ways, as well as those who engage in such practices.

The similarities and differences between political and ethical *parrhēsia* I have identified raise the question of exactly what it means to risk one's life. In light of Foucault's and my own analyses of militant Cynic ethical *parrhēsia*, I identify three possible meanings. First, a practitioner of either political or ethical *parrhēsia* might be killed by another person because of the uncomfortable truths they reveal. (Just as Plato incurred the murderous wrath of Dionysus, it's possible that Diogenes could have provoked someone to the point of wanting to take his life.) Second, in the case of the Cynics, by rejecting basic protections that help to keep human beings alive, the ethical parrhesiast increases their chances of dying of, for example, disease or hunger, or of succumbing due to the elements. Third, both political and ethical parrhesiasts can be said to risk their lives through calling into question their own ontological status; they risk becoming unintelligible as lives – even as lives that are not fully or at all livable. In Butler's terms, they risk not only lack of recognition but also lack of apprehension, such that their reduction to subhumanity and degrading treatment – their reduction to humiliation – would be not ignored or normalized but merely unintelligible by any measure (Butler 2010).[15] In light of the connection I have drawn between militant Cynic ethical *parrhēsia* and the countering of sexual humiliation, the terms in which Foucault describes the Cynics' risking of their lives are instructive. It is the "exposed" character of the Cynics' existence that puts them at risk, where "exposure" is synonymous with "display." Yet Foucault illustrates that it is through the risk resulting from that exposure and display that transformation becomes possible. The same is true for victims/survivors of sexual violence who risk their lives by exposing and displaying themselves in ways that confront and subvert the humiliation that exposes and displays them before themselves as subhuman, less than fully livable lives deserving of being treated as if they were nonhuman. "[I]t seems," Butler writes,

> that power acts upon the body, specifically, in the very formulation
> of bodily passion . . . by which we affectively seize upon or release a

fundamental sense of identity. The body in some ways becomes passion in this reformulation, a passion for my own being which must pass
through what is Other, the condition of my reflexivity in which I undergo
those norms over which I have no choice. It is also, however, in that undergoing that I stand a chance of discovering some other way to be.

(2004, 193)

I have argued that SlutWalk and MPCW protesters (which include,
albeit not in the same ways, both individuals who offer help and Sulkowicz
herself) risk their lives in the third sense described above. Through calling into question the conditions for the possibility of their intelligibility,
they risk becoming unintelligible as lives – livable or otherwise.[16] Risking
unintelligibility through exposing and challenging normalizing norms elucidates the relevance of the second way of risking one's life identified above.
When victims/survivors subvert humiliation, like the Cynics, they forego
ontological comfort; they take up Nietzsche's challenge to engage the possibility of meaninglessness rather than accept meaning that renders life,
and therefore oneself, merely "worthless." This subversion also disrupts the
normalizing, scripted, gendered response to sexual violence. As illustrated
throughout this book, women who refuse to be "properly" gendered, who
expose and challenge the harms of gendered relations of power, forego the
protections femininity affords. Like the Cynics, the precarity of their existence increases; they become "differentially exposed to injury, violence, and
death" (Butler 2010, 25). Foucault shows us that in constituting ourselves
in terms of and therefore binding ourselves to oppositional, subjugated, uncomfortable truths, we simultaneously constitute ourselves in terms of risk
and, hence in terms of courage, possibility, difference, and transformation.
While risking their lives in each of the three ways I have described further
distances the Cynic from the rest of humanity, on Foucault's reading, it is
precisely by means of standing apart from them that the Cynic comes into
solidarity with others. This is a solidarity that resonates with the relation
of self-to-self to which militancy bears witness: it breaks with convention
in ways that are not merely destructive but which rather cultivate difference
and possibility. In the next, concluding chapter of this book, I explore what
such a form of solidarity might look like, as well as its counter-normalizing/
counter-humiliating, feminist implications.

Notes

1 At this time, democracy and *parrhēsia* came to both mutually condition and
threaten one another. On the one hand, *parrhēsia* required democracy because
democracy was a condition for the possibility of truth. "[T]here can only be
true discourse," Foucault explains, "and access to true discourse for everybody
where there is democracy." At the same time, the reality that not everyone
will in fact speak the truth introduces a "difference" among citizens that is by
nature hierarchical (a few are truth-tellers, some are merely flatterers, while

others are liars) and therefore incompatible with the democratic principle of equality: "there can only be true discourse through democracy, but true discourse introduces something completely different and irreducible to the egalitarian structure of democracy." On the other hand, *parrhēsia* is a condition for the possibility of democracy because it is true discourse that will sustain a democratic society through any "misadventures, events, jousts, and wars" it may experience. Democracy, however, seeks to avoid the very "joust . . . conflict . . . confrontation . . . and rivalry" through which truth emerges. In sum, then, there is "no true discourse without democracy, but true discourse introduces difference into democracy. No democracy without true discourse, but democracy threatens the very existence of true discourse" (2010, 184).

2　Foucault explains: "I do not mean – and we must be very clear about this – that *parrhēsia*, truth-telling disappeared from the field of politics" (2010, 340).

3　Foucault's analysis here provides important insight into the self-renunciation, obedience, and conformity that characterize the early Christian self-relation and which, he argues, are inherited by modern Western subjectivity as a mode of self-relation.

4　Some of Sulkowicz's more recent performance art/protest pieces have generated controversy (see da Silva 2017 and Yang 2017).

5　Louise du Toit also identifies public exposure of women's bodies as disrupting the seamless reproduction of norms that create the conditions under which sexual violence occurs and is regularized. Although her argument in this regard is made by way of analyzing a literary text, it is grounded in and in turn supports her philosophical analyses. Du Toit analyzes a scene from Lindsay Colleen's novel, *The Rape of Sita*, in which two women, Sibyl and Alexsina, are detained by male police officers following a political protest. In order to teach them their place (the private rather than public realm), the police took them away in a Jeep to gang rape them. The women responded by standing up in the back of the Jeep, loudly ridiculing the policemen precisely as men, tearing their own clothes off, and challenging the men to get on with the rape. The police "got scared, started to giggle, lost their nerve, and took the women back to the city" (2009, 214). Du Toit contends that the women effectively disrupted the normative and normalizing scripting of rape. They "refused to be silenced;" they "asserted themselves" in their gendered and embodied self-relations; and they pre-empted the men by removing their own clothing, publicly exposing and displaying parts of the body normed as private and thus needing to be covered (Ibid). Also significant in du Toit's view, and from my own as I shall discuss later, is the fact that the women acted together, "in solidarity" (Ibid).

　　Namrata Mitra describes an actual, organized anti-rape protest that possesses important similarities and, therefore, effects to the fictionalized one described by du Toit. As Mitra describes it, in response to the gang rape of a thirty-two-year-old woman by the Indian army, 'a group of older Manipuri women activists called Meira Paibi, or "Torch Bearers,"' staged a protest outside of military headquarters. The women protested naked, and carried a banner reading (in red lettering) "Indian Army Rape Us." The women also chanted, "We mothers have come. Drink our blood. Eat our flesh. Maybe this way you can spare our daughters" (2018, 197–198). Like the fictionalized, spontaneous protest du Toit describes, this organized protest by Indian women is public and embodied, the women refused to be silenced, they appeared naked, they called out the men, and they appeared as a group in solidarity with one another. While du Toit notes that the incident described in the novel occurred within the context of a matriarchal culture, this is clearly not the case with the incident Mitra describes; indeed, her essay is dedicated to elucidating and analyzing the sexism and misogyny within India (see du Toit 2009 and Mitra 2018).

6 The letter's authors conclude it with an expression of solidarity that is simultaneously a call for intersectional feminist activism:

> Sisters from Toronto, rape and sexual assault is a radical weapon of oppression and we are in full agreement that it requires radical people and radical strategies to counter it. In that spirit, and because there is so much work to be done and great potential to do it together, we ask that the SlutWalk be even more radical and break from what has historically been the erasure of Black women and their particular needs, their struggles as well as their potential and contributions to feminist movements and all other movements.

Susan Brison posted the letter in its entirety to the Huffington Post and also expressed solidarity with its authors (see Brison 2011).

7 I am grateful to Qrescent Mason for bringing Rose's activist work to my attention.

8 I am not suggesting that all SlutWalk protesters have the experience I describe. My point is not that the protests necessarily entail but rather that they open onto counter-normalizing/counter-humiliating modes of experiencing one's relationship to oneself and therefore to others and world.

9 As I discuss in Chapter 5, some of these same techniques, including manner of dress and using the body as a written text, were deployed in protests against Brett Kavanaugh's appointment to the U.S. Supreme Court and in support of Christine Blasey Ford.

10 Consistent with my analysis in this chapter, Sharon Marcus's account of rape as a scripted act identifies the cultivation by women of subversive forms of embodiment as key to disrupting that script and thus countering sexual violence. Marcus argues, and I agree with her, that women need to develop modes of embodied self-relation that possess the capacity to respond with physical violence to sexually violent attacks. See Marcus 1992.

11 Rebecca Mead (2015) provides a provocative feminist analysis of MPCW.

12 Sulkowicz and four of her friends carried the mattress across the stage at Columbia's 2015 graduation ceremony (see Taylor 2015).

13 Sulkowicz developed particular "rules of engagement" for the performance/protest. These included: (1) She must carry the mattress with her whenever she is on any Columbia University property; (2) She must have the mattress with her whenever she is inside a "Columbia University owned-building"; (3) She may not ask for help carrying the mattress but may accept it if it is offered – this includes allowing someone who offers to carry the mattress for her; (4) She must leave the mattress "in a safe place on campus" when leaving the Columbia campus; (5) When returning to campus she must immediately retrieve the mattress from wherever she left it (see Smith 2014).

14 Mead notes that on Columbia's campus, students organized "collective carries" with multiple participants, as well as that anti-sexual violence protests on other campuses have utilized mattresses (see Mead 2015). Consistent with Mead's characterization of them, these offers of help resonate with gestures of solidarity as I present them in Chapter 5.

15 Butler identifies apprehension as the basis for critique, insofar as it enables realization of the fact that "something is not recognized by recognition" (2010, 5).

16 Foucault's analysis of the Cynics illustrates that risking one's life in this ontological sense may in fact entail risking it in the first sense. The Cynics were subjected to verbal and physical abuse, the latter of which could have resulted in death. SlutWalk participants have been and Sulkowicz was subjected to verbal harassment and abuse, and anyone who engages in public political protest, especially members of marginalized groups who expose as normalizing and thereby threaten existing relations of power, is vulnerable to physical attack.

Conclusion
Gestures of solidarity

During the summer of 2017, I participated in a National Endowment for the Humanities (NEH) Institute, the theme of which was Diverse Philosophical Perspectives on Sexual Violence. The intellectual work I did during those two weeks moved this book forward in important ways; the value of that work can itself be attributed in large part to connections I forged with other participants. Returning to my dorm room one afternoon, brain buzzing from the day's meetings, the phrase "embodied gestures of solidarity" popped into my head, and I scribbled it down on a pad of paper. I was not at all sure what I meant by the phrase, but it resonated and I knew I wanted to explore it.

As I will discuss in the concluding remarks that follow, the notion of embodied gestures of solidarity can be seen as a response to the philosophical and practical problems that preoccupied me during the Institute's two weeks, and which I have elucidated and analyzed in this book. The initial appeal of specifically "embodied" gestures stemmed from my concerns about how the limits and failures of normative language, communicability, and meaning-making generally, as well as the normalizing exploitation of those limitations and failures within the context of gendered relations of power, complicate and even silence women's articulation of their experiences of sexual violence and thus reinforce systemic sexism and misogyny. I had started to wonder, especially since sexual violence is an embodied violation, whether bodies could perhaps in some way express not only the experience of sexual violence, but also those limitations and failures – could express sexual violence as an experience that, while it is neither unintelligible nor incommunicable, nonetheless cannot be, as I noted in Chapter 1, *fully* conceptualized or *fully* communicated. The notion of gesture also seemed to facilitate exploration of such expression by and between individuals within the context of daily life. In light of the ubiquity of normalization – its infiltration of the minutiae of existence – effective counter-normalization, it seemed to me, not only needed to but in fact could occur and must already be occurring in and through mundane, routine practices. I had, in turn, begun to see solidarity as a condition for the possibility of a kind of gesture that could function in the counter-normalizing and therefore counter-humiliating manner I envisioned.

While I have subsequently learned that gesture by definition encompasses bodily (including verbal) expression, I think, ultimately, that the phrase "embodied gestures of solidarity" captured something I discerned within certain encounters and exchanges I had at the NEH Institute, encounters and exchanges in which experiences of sexual violence and humiliation (including my own) were conveyed and acknowledged in simultaneously affirmative and transformative ways. In what follows, I endeavor to sketch out more fully the nature of counter-normalizing/counter-humiliating gestures of solidarity, gestures characterized by affirmation that simultaneously calls into question, individuation that also extends beyond, reaching out that is taking in, coming together that occurs through loosening attachments. They are gestures of shared transformative disclosure, the effects of which cannot be known in advance. The risking of self-attachment they both convey and generate provides the basis for broader transformative modes of connection and engagement. These gestures are micro-level, individual but not individuating, bodily expressions; their effects are not, however, insignificant. I locate the significance of a gesture within what it contains and conveys, not within the scope of its reach.

I

In *Notes Toward a Performative Theory of Assembly*, Judith Butler suggests that a shared experience of precarity has the potential to function as a condition for the possibility of solidarity. "In our individual vulnerability to a precarity that is socially induced," Butler writes,

> each "I" potentially sees how its unique sense of anxiety and failures has been implicated all along in a broader social world. This initiates the possibility of taking apart that individualizing and maddening form of responsibility in favor of an ethos of solidarity that would affirm mutual dependency . . . and open the way to a form of improvisation in the course of devising collective and institutional ways of addressing induced precarity.
>
> (2015, 21–22)

For Butler, the realization that the source of one's differential experience of openness and exposure, as well as the differential experience of injury that results, is an effect of prevailing relations of power rather than of one's own inadequacies can provide the basis for aligning with others whose lives are likewise characterized by precarity. Solidarity, from her perspective, asserts and affirms the interconnection of the self-relation with relations to others and world. It is characterized by coming and being together with others that is forged through a common, shared experience of openness and exposure and, by extension, of uncertainty and risk. Inter-relationality thus takes the form of a mutual becoming otherwise, where connection with another is made through shared loosening of self-attachments. It entails unpredictably transformative disclosure. As Butler explains in an interview with Sara Ahmed, "deviation . . . undertaken in concert with others" facilitates "new forms of solidarity that make it possible to risk a new sense of being a subject" (Ahmed 2016, 488). Consistent, moreover, with her characterization of precariousness and precarity in terms of embodiment (recall her assertion that bodies come up against and therefore impinge upon and are impinged upon by one another), Butler also consistently emphasizes that it is specifically as bodies that we assemble and act together. "Solidarity," she contends, is "a gathering enacted by bodies under duress or in the name of duress, where the gathering itself signifies persistence and resistance" (2015, 23).

Gesture as Maurice Merleau-Ponty conceives of it possesses the same character of embodied transformative disclosure that Butler locates within solidarity. "Expressive" embodied "action that signifies," gestures convey meaning through their dual character of sedimentation and spontaneity (Cuffari 2016, 234). Sedimentation refers to the fact that gestures emerge from, only make sense within, and therefore derive their intelligibility from a context of shared understanding.[1] This context may be broad (the society in which one lives) or as specific as one's own dwelling space.[2] Spontaneity points to the dynamic and therefore unpredictable nature of gestures. Neither language nor modes of embodiment remain static over time, and numerous variations exist within and across normatively enacted and recognizable gestures. The simultaneity of sedimentation and spontaneity is apparent in the fact that meaning is not distinct from but rather contained within a gesture, that gestures are not simply expressions of universal concepts or "psychic facts" that precede and are therefore necessary for their interpretation (Merleau-Ponty 1966, 184). "It is through my body," Merleau-Ponty asserts, 'that I perceive "things." The meaning of a gesture thus "understood" is not behind it, it intermingles with the structure of the world outlined by the gesture, which I take up on my own account' (186). The particular combinations of bodily comportment, facial expression, and tone of voice that comprise gestures, in other words, acquire meaning and are thus recognized only within a broader socio-cultural context. "The gesture *does not make me think* of anger," Merleau-Ponty writes, "it is anger itself" (184; original emphasis).[3] Yet because no two individuals within a given context will manifest the embodiment of anger in exactly the same way (my face might become red when I am angry while yours turns pale), it is the broader "structure of the world" that lends to our different gestures intelligibility in the precise form of anger.

The transformative and disclosive character of gesture stems from the simultaneity of sedimentation and spontaneity Merleau-Ponty describes. Insofar as the social intelligibility of a gesture depends upon its manifestation within and across particular bodies, singular meaning ("anger") can be expressed only through multiplicity and therefore variation; at the same time, because their intelligibility also depends upon their implication within a broader social context, gestures always exceed the limits and intentions of those particular embodied manifestations. Just as they unsettle normative notions of general and particular, given and contingent, ground and effect, gestures likewise reflect the interconnection of the relation of self to self with relations to others and world. This unsettling and reflection open onto possibilities for alternative ways of conceptualizing and living embodied self-self and self-other relations. Gestures are neither individuating nor internalizing. They reflect back toward the self-relation at the same time that they reach out into the world; they reflect a shared understanding at the same time that they transform it. Tellingly, Merleau-Ponty characterizes the transformative coming and being together that gestures both contain and open onto in the same terms Butler uses to describe solidarity: such inter-relational transformation, he contends, is apparent in the *improvisation* of the artist. Unlike the self-referential improvisation of the child prodigy, the improvisation of the artist extends outward, "toward the world;" a "bridge to the other," it appeals to as yet unrealized possibility (Merleau-Ponty 1973, 56).

The transformative bridging that characterizes improvisation is disclosive. Merleau-Ponty describes gestures' function of both reflecting and extending beyond the self-relation in terms of a simultaneity of "receiving and giving" (1973, 11). In the gesture of reading a book, for example, one receives and therefore takes in what the author has written; at the same time, one's reading of a text is always framed by one's own "experience of others and everyday events," such that author and text "come to dwell in [the reader's] world" (Ibid). Just as the author of a text discloses themself through their writing, so the reader discloses through what they bring to their reading. Merleau-Ponty describes here an extension of the self-relation that reaches out to others, and which does so in a way that invites them in. Gestures are thus not merely self-expression; they make a request. As Butler puts it, "action and gesture signify and speak, both as action and claim; the one is not finally extricable from the other" (2015, 83). The very notion of a request contains within it an appeal for reception, and it is through this appeal that gesture (mutually) discloses. Inviting you to dinner at my home conveys the fact that I enjoy and therefore desire, or am perhaps in need of, your company. This disclosure of a desire or need exposes me through its appeal to be received and responded to. At the same time, being prevailed upon to receive and respond exposes you; whether or not you receive the appeal and whether and how you respond to it functions as self-disclosure on your part. Merleau-Ponty makes clear, moreover, that the disclosive nature of gesture is itself improvisational and, therefore, transformative. The book one reads, he writes, "makes use of everything I have contributed in order to carry me beyond it" (1973, 11). The author "varies the ordinary meaning of the signs, and like a whirlwind they sweep me along toward another meaning with which I am going to connect" (12).

Construed in terms of these notions of solidarity and gesture, gestures of solidarity as I conceive of them are counter-normalizing. As a mode of human inter-relationality that reflects the interconnection of the self-relation with relations to others and world and affirms as the basis for those relations the openness and exposure that characterize their interconnection, such gestures oppose internalization and individuation. Just as the counter-normalizing modes of self-relation described in previous chapters are characterized by assertion of self that is at the same time self-transformative, so do gestures of solidarity reflect a way of coming together with others that is at the same time a mutual becoming otherwise. These gestures entail mutually transformative (self)disclosure in which ontological status and self-attachments are asserted through being, respectively, risked and loosened. Openness and mutual dependency are asserted, transformative disclosure is enacted, and coming- and being-together occurs, moreover, in specifically embodied ways. Gestures of solidarity reflect "a generosity which is not a compromise with the adversity of the world and which is on [one's] side against it" (Merleau-Ponty 1963, 25–26).

II

While gestures of solidarity might be cultivated within a variety of daily practices and interactions in a variety of ways, I want to focus on their counter-normalizing and counter-humiliating effects relative to the specific problem with which I opened the book, and which underpins its arguments and analyses: the struggle of victims/survivors to make sense of and meaningfully articulate their experiences of sexual violence; their struggle to achieve unambiguous recognition of rape and sexual assault as harms; and their struggle to themselves be fully recognized and thereby not reduced to either the experience of sexual violence or these struggles. Gestures of solidarity, in my view, both reflect and facilitate counter-normalizing/counter-humiliating navigation of the current sociopolitical landscape – the gendered relations of power – that gives rise to sexual violence and promotes the ambivalence in the face of it that exploits limitations and thereby fosters failure of meaning-making, expression, and communication. These gestures critically confront gendered power relations in the sense that they acknowledge and proceed on the basis of rather than disavow or evade the reality that the experience of sexual violence is not fully conceptualizable. Foregrounding the interconnection of self-relation and other/world relations, gestures of solidarity do not attribute failures of expression and communication to either individual victims/survivors or individual interlocutors; nor, then, do they promote internalization of such failures. Rather, the gestures situate limitations and failures of language, communicability, and meaning-making within gendered power relations and, as counter-normalizing/humiliating interventions within those power relations, challenge them. Ultimately, gestures of solidarity (continue to) reach out into a reality where few people are going to "get it," while at the same time refusing to allow this reality to become an intractable barrier to meaningful, transformative, affirmative inter-relationality. Such gestures convey that transmitting meaning from sexual violence to after, creating a bridge to the other, is possible only through reaching out into a space of failed testimony, as well as a willingness to do so over and over again.[4] As Sandra Bartky asserts, the demand to try and "get it" is a demand for a *transformative* knowing – a knowing that in transforming "the self who knows" generates not merely "new cognitions" but also "new affects" (2002, 71–72).

As my analyses in previous chapters make clear, there is no normative experience of sexual humiliation, internalization and individuation do not manifest in the same way within the self-relations of any two victims/survivors, nor is the nature of that manifestation static. I have gained a sense of what kinds of interactions counter my own experience of sexual humiliation only over time and through a process of elimination. Sympathy alone makes me feel worse. I experience someone being sorry for me as both individuating and internalizing; it reduces the violation that was inflicted against me to me and leaves it there. Sympathy coupled with indignation and outrage, by contrast, feels like a gesture of solidarity. Such a response conveys that what was done to me was wrong – a wrong committed by another against me – and recognizes or is at least willing to try and understand the nature of that wrongness (and its effects). It also recognizes the risk and exposure that characterize disclosures of experiences of sexual violence, recognition that in turn reflects a willingness to be exposed; ultimately, it is a response that reflects commitment to remain in that place of exposure, to deal with the discomfort it inevitably generates, and to allow oneself to become different together with someone else through that experience. Sympathetic outrage doesn't reduce what happened to me, to me or, therefore, reduce me to my own sexual humiliation; in that way, and consistent with gestures of solidarity, it constitutes a disclosive transformation with broader counter-normalizing/counter-humiliating implications.

Having kept my own experience of sexual violence mostly to myself, I haven't had many opportunities to experience gestures of solidarity. Occasions upon which I have therefore tend to stand out in my mind. A few days into the NEH Institute, I told a friend that I had been raped. Intimate friendship, in which people reveal their "deep secrets whose exposure to the public eye would make [them] extremely vulnerable," according to Avishai Margalit, is one of the most serious casualties of humiliation (1996, 209). As discussed in Chapter 2, Margalit contends that humiliating treatment both deprives its targets of control and impresses upon them this truncated or nonexistent ability to participate in shaping the conditions of their existence. Being denied a realm of privacy, denial that occurs by means of the imposed exposure before oneself and others as subhuman that humiliation entails, is a key aspect of this lack or denial of control. Insofar as privacy is a necessary condition for the possibility of intimacy, Margalit argues that humiliation seriously inhibits the formation of friendship, one of the most "significant" of all "belonging relationships" (208).[5]

My friend and I didn't discuss my experience at length when I told her about it, nor did we talk about it again during the ensuing days. We did, however, develop routines that we sustained for the duration of the Institute. We met most mornings and picked up coffees before walking together to daily seminar meetings, and we shopped for food and prepared simple evening meals at a communal kitchen that was available for Institute participants' use. I experienced shopping, cooking, and eating dinner together, in particular, as a gesture of solidarity. The embodied practices of examining produce in the grocery store, navigating the automatic checkout machines that inevitably failed to work, chopping vegetables in the kitchen over a beer, stirring things on the stove, sitting across the table from one another, washing pots and loading the dishwasher, was how my friend and I reached out toward one another, into the space of limited meaning-making and failed testimony. These activities were all *shared* and although, again, we never made this explicit, I experienced them as being intentionally so. My friend and I didn't divide up tasks – one of us selecting vegetables while the other chose beer, one of us chopping vegetables while the other sautéed; we both did all of these things together. Although our bodies never actually came into direct contact, we handled the same fruits and vegetables, the same cooking implements, we occupied the same spaces in proximity to one another. We created a space characterized by the simultaneity of intimacy and lack.

This space and the embodied practices that generated and occurred within it were transformative and disclosive, sedimented and spontaneous. Obviously tasks each of us had performed numerous times and readily recognized as being part of meal preparation, within the context of that particular kitchen, those particular two weeks, these simple practices were also bridges – continual, improvisational, partial, *bridgings* to one another that expressed mutual recognition of our own limits and mutual commitment to the ongoing traversing of those limits in new ways and, hence, to one another. Nonverbal gestures of solidarity can take even simpler forms. Extending a hand – a reach that does not become touch – can convey desire to understand and to help infused with recognition of a constrained ability to do so. I have discerned in certain combinations of facial expressions, bodily comportment, and emotional sounds (i.e., a sigh, a sharp inhalation or exhalation of breath, a low rumble in the back of the throat) anger tinged with frustration and even grief in the face of deep seated and intransigent systemic sexism and misogyny, the depth of the injury sexual violence inflicts, and the far-reaching effects and ramifications of that injury.

The gestures of solidarity I have noted here convey that the space of limited meaning and failed testimony can never be fully or finally bridged, express sorrow in the face of this, and direct that sorrow toward a mutual commitment to not give up trying; they convey a receiving that is simultaneously a giving, a taking in and an extending back toward what has been offered. As embodied, moreover, these gestures undermine (sexual) stigmatization. They express mutual affirmation of openness and exposure, recognition of and commitment to continuing to navigate the fraught process of trying to make sense of and communicate experiences of sexual violence, and willingness to be transformed in unforeseen ways. The mutual taking on of risk and, therefore, the courage it reflects, assert and affirm the open, exposed, embodied self-relations of both parties. This shared recognition and experience redirects openness and exposure outward and therefore opens onto their transformation. Especially in the case of victims/survivors, this transformation may entail an experience of the interconnection of the self-relation with relations to others and world not merely as a susceptibility to violation but also as a ground for an intimacy that is defined by improvisation and, thus, a mutual becoming other. Ultimately, I see gestures of solidarity functioning as the limit manifestation of prevailing responses to sexual violence. There is no scandalous, public reversal here, but there is a laying bare of – a bearing witness to – the thoughtless conventionality of prevailing responses to victims/survivors who endeavor to convey and be validated in their experiences and their responses to those experiences, whatever form those articulations and responses take. Sexual humiliation, as I have shown, (re)produces silence and the conditions for its possibility. The intimacy that fosters conditions under which it is possible to counter that silencing, to perform the ongoing work of endeavoring to meaningfully express and receive what leaves one most exposed and open, need not and, as I have also shown, cannot be undertaken only through words.

I have noted that, given the nature and function of normalizing power, I am primarily concerned with how gestures of solidarity can be cultivated inter-relationally within the context of everyday lived experience. At the same time, these gestures have a place within the context of feminist anti-sexual violence political action and protest. As Tarana Burke deploys it in her activist work with young victims/survivors of color, the statement "Me Too" functions as exactly the sort of transformative reaching out/taking in that characterizes gestures of solidarity. The speaker is exposed through a disclosure of victimization that makes an appeal for support. Her interlocutor is exposed through being prevailed upon to provide that support as well as, within this particular context, through perhaps identifying herself as a victim/survivor. This shared exposure is a disclosure of self that is at the same time an extension beyond self in ways that risk self-attachment. It provides the basis for mutually transformative interactions between interlocutors. There is no guarantee either that the appeal by the speaker of the words "Me Too" will be taken up, or that it will be taken up in ways that generate externalization and inter-relationality such that the cycle of self-assertion and -renunciation that characterizes sexual humiliation is disrupted and alternatives are opened onto. At the same time, implicit in the statement is a commitment to acknowledge, validate, and support the disclosure of other victims/survivors; it is an appeal that contains within itself the conditions for the reception of that appeal. Moreover, and significant in light of my reservations about #MeToo, the statement "Me Too" makes it possible to meaningfully disclose an experience of sexual violence without having to do so publicly or in detail.[6] Burke has expressed concern that the emphasis on particular (as well as high-profile) individuals and their stories within the context of #MeToo has conveyed to victims/survivors that an experience of sexual violation is not "valid" unless the specifics of it have been related publicly.[7] "What we're trying to do," she asserts,

> is counter that narrative and say, "You don't have to tell your story publicly. You don't have to tell anybody what happened to you." You have to get it out — but it doesn't have to be at a poetry reading. It doesn't have to be on social media . . . It's like a balancing act because I have to acknowledge that stories are important, and sometimes saying the words, "This happened to me" and "This is what he did" is cathartic to get out. I think there's enough evidence in this world of survival and recovery to show that repeating that doesn't help you, though. Reliving that doesn't help you.
>
> (Harris 2018)

Burke relates a story that captures the essence of "Me Too" as a gesture of solidarity. She explains that after #MeToo emerged, numerous people encouraged her to create and sell t-shirts emblazoned with the phrase as a way to generate funds for her organization. Such shirts have, in fact, existed for years. "We don't sell the t-shirts," Burke explains, 'because they are a gift. A lot of times I hand them out and say: "Whenever you're ready"' (Brockes 2018). Whether or not Burke actually says anything, handing a "MeToo" shirt to another, similar to reaching out a hand in a manner akin to that which I described above, constitutes an extension of her body toward another person. This embodied reaching out toward takes the form of a simultaneous giving and receiving, an invitation that is also an appeal, an expression and disclosure of herself through risking herself that mutually implicates the other. This invitation, moreover, is open-ended: "*Whenever you're ready.*"

Gestures of solidarity also have a place within feminist anti-sexual violence protest. They are apparent in two ways within the protests that occurred during the Kavanaugh hearings.[8] First, the protests generated inter-relational gestures of solidarity that opened onto broader political action. On the Friday morning of the Senate Judiciary Committee's vote to advance Kavanaugh's nomination to the full Senate, Maria Gallagher was among the protesters gathered in the Hart Senate Building.[9] She was there by herself, and since she had not participated in the protests that had taken place throughout the week, she didn't have a clear idea of how best to contribute (Wilde 2019). Someone eventually asked her if she wanted to go wait in front of Senator Jeff Flake's office. Flake was considered a swing vote in advancing Kavanaugh's candidacy and, should he appear, Gallagher was instructed to encourage him to vote no. Having also been told to "bring a friend," Gallagher went in search of one, which is how she met Ana Maria Archila (Ibid). Co-executive Director of the Center for Popular Democracy, Archila had participated in organizing and been involved in the protests all week; in fact, she had for the first time given a public account of her experience of childhood sexual assault in front of Flake's office (Vesoulis 2018; Wilde 2019).

Gallagher and Archila are the two women who confronted Flake on an elevator as he was attempting to get from his office to the Judiciary Committee hearings. That confrontation in many ways personifies the characteristics of ontologically risky, counter-normalizing/counter-humiliating practice as I describe it in Chapter 3. The two women, both victims/survivors, publicly challenged a figure who, if not the actual source of their sexual humiliation, is a representation of the gendered relations of power that, in their production and legitimation of sexual violence against women, allowed Kavanaugh to be confirmed despite Ford's allegations against him. In confronting Flake, Gallagher and Archila publicly stated that they had been sexually violated, asserted the truth of that violation, and therefore constituted themselves in terms of it. Their speaking was characterized by risk: they had no idea how Flake would respond; whether they would be arrested for blocking the elevator; or how they would be affected after the fact, given that the incident was being recorded by television cameras. One of the most powerful expressions of the turning back of their sexual humiliation against its source is Gallagher's demand that Flake look at her when she speaks. She demands that he recognize her as the embodiment of women's subhumanization and their treatment as if nonhuman through acts of sexual violence, and that he recognize his complicity in both should he vote in favor of Kavanaugh's appointment. "You're telling all women that they don't matter, that they should just stay quiet, because if they tell you what happened to them you're going to ignore them," Gallagher asserted, her voice shaking with emotion. "That's what you're telling me right now," she continued. "Look at me when I'm talking to you . . . don't turn away from me!" (Malveaux and Stracqualursi 2018).

Gallagher and Archila's confrontation of Flake is also a gesture of solidarity made between the two women. These strangers reached out toward one another across the space of failed testimony and limited meaning-making. They created the intimacy of friendship through transformative disclosure, a mutual loosening of self-attachments. Coming together through becoming other to themselves, their actions open onto possibilities for "an other life in *this* world" (Foucault 2011, 319; original emphasis).

The Kavanaugh protests also offer insight into what broader, collective gestures of solidarity might look like. The protests' overtly embodied character reflects that of SlutWalks and MPCW. As in SlutWalks, the body was used as a text and mode of dress was intentionally and subversively deployed. Protesters wrote on their hands and faces, as well as covered their mouths with black tape displaying, statements such as, "Believe," "I Believe," "Believe Survivors," and "Be a Hero;" some expressions mentioned or directly addressed Christine Blasey Ford: "I Believe Christine," "We Believe You." Raised fists were a recurring gesture. With respect to dress, most protesters wore black garments, including t- shirts bearing the above-noted and similar sentiments; one group of women donned the red robes and white bonnets worn by women in the television version of *The Handmaid's Tale*. The way in which bodies occupied space and the particular spaces they occupied was also significant. Protests (and arrests) took place outside the offices of individual Senators, as well as outside and within the room where the hearings were held. A National Walkout in support of Ford was held on September 24th, 2018. Groups of protesters across the U.S., wearing black clothing, gathered wherever they happened to be from 1 to 2 pm, Eastern time. In Washington, D.C., protesters met at the Capitol and marched (many with fists raised) to the Supreme Court, in front of which they held a sit-in and speakout.

While they may not entail the intentional taking on of humiliation that is apparent in Gallagher's and Archila's actions, in their opposition to Kavanaugh, the protests certainly sought to turn the humiliation of sexual violence back against its source. It is in their more specific expression of support for Christine Blasey Ford, however, that the protests can be seen to reflect collective gestures of solidarity. Broadly, they contain the combination of anger and compassion that, as I have noted, I perceive in such gestures. More specifically, the protests draw attention to the power relations that produce failed testimony and exacerbate limited meaning making and communication and, therefore, to that failure and those limits themselves. Taped mouths emulate victims'/survivors' silencing, in the face of which statements on the tape express outrage and grief. These protests reach out into the space of failed testimony and curtailed meaning with gestures that are simultaneously defiant and deeply compassionate; they reach out with raised voices, raised fists, as well as with tears. "What does it mean," Butler writes,

> to act together when the conditions for acting together are devastated or falling away? Such an impasse can become the paradoxical condition of a form of social solidarity both mournful and joyful, a gathering enacted by bodies under duress or in the name of duress, where the gathering itself signifies persistence and resistance.
>
> (2015, 23)

III

"We do not," Bartky writes, "share the sufferings of those with whom we want to stand in solidarity. Their suffering is the intentional object to which our commiseration . . . is directed. While there are points of similarly between a feeling and that feeling commiserated-with . . . *the two are not identical*. I commiserate with your sufferings and take joy in your joys" but I do not experience them; "they are *yours*" (2002, 81; original emphasis).

The distinction Bartky marks between experiencing and feeling what another does and endeavoring to make sense of and respond to their experiences and feelings points to the never fully commensurable nature of ways of being in the world. This incommensurability once again foregrounds the ubiquity of limited meaning making and communicability as well as, in the case of victims/survivors, the space of failed testimony. In light of this incommensurability and ubiquity, it seems to me that continually reasserting and confronting the impossibilities of experiencing and feeling what another experiences and feels needs to be considered a necessary component of, rather than a barrier to, counter-normalizing/counter-humiliating disclosive and transformative encounters. Such continual assertion and confrontation of these impossibilities needs to be considered, in other words, a condition for the possibility of not only gestures of solidarity, but also of political solidarity more broadly.

At the same time that she points to the ongoing, incomplete, potentially fraught bridgings that characterize gestures of solidarity, Bartky expresses an (albeit somewhat wistful) desire to get beyond or bring to an end such a process. Second Wave feminists, she writes, "were wrong or even arrogant in having believed that we had already achieved sisterhood" (2002, 79). She also argues, however, that the Second Wave was "surely wrong too in allowing ourselves to be shamed" for having been "committed" to such a notion "at all" (Ibid). Gestures of solidarity, and any sort of feminist activism or politics onto which they might open or of which they might be part, point to the need for critical engagement with that to which such a commitment appeals. Bartky appeals to both love and "yearning for a more solidary world" (Ibid). In light of what I have presented in this book concerning normalizing gendered relations of power, sexual violence, and sexual humiliation, the commitments reflected in gestures of solidarity – to risk, to keep risking, to be willing to change – may seem insufficiently bold. I think, however, that the counter-normalizing/counter-humiliating potential of these gestures, and the commitments they (re)assert by refusing to allow the space of limited meaning making and failed testimony to function as a barrier to making transformative connections with others, are real and significant. By elucidating the inevitability of this space, gestures of solidarity point to the need to confront, grapple with, and work to create ways of coming together in the face of the space and its inevitability, rather than either retreating or attempting to eradicate them. Gestures of solidarity are ongoing because the space of limited meaning making and failed testimony is continually reproduced by normalizing power relations in their multiple and interlocking permutations.

The perpetual work gestures of solidarity require may itself function as a barrier to counter-normalization. It may generate feelings of futility, it may lead to exhaustion; ultimately, it may simply make people give up. At the same time, along with the capacities of intimacy and commitment, gestures of solidarity can cultivate perseverance and patience. In many ways, the embodiment of these capacities, Burke has made clear that her focus is less on the current moment than on putting the moment to work, deploying it to counter sexual violence and the conditions for its possibility. What is important about attention and privilege, she asserts, is using it in

> the service of other people . . . Now that I have it, I'm trying to use it responsibly . . . but if it hadn't come along I would be right here, with my fucking Me Too shirt on, doing workshops and going to rape crisis centers. The work is the work.
>
> (Brockes 2018)

Burke's comments echo Foucault's view that patience, perseverance, commitment, as well as intimacy, are themselves critical and creative capacities that function as the work of freedom. I think, moreover, that he in fact considered these capacities to be quite bold. The reality of normalization as Foucault presents it is simultaneously discouraging and heartening. He makes clear that the effects of normalization are extensive, but in doing so, he also illustrates that what has not yet been thought or imagined is equally so. It is a reality that shows us as feminists just how much work there is to be done, but it also shows us that there are multiple opportunities for carrying out that work and provides us with valuable tools for doing so. The fact that this work of freedom is continual does not mean, as Foucault reminds us, that it can only be done in "disorder and contingency" (Foucault 1980c, 47). It is precisely this ongoing public, critical, risky, disruptive, unsettling, uncertain, making possible, the becoming other than what we currently are in terms of self-relation and other/world relations, that constitutes the "patient labor" that "giv[es] form to our impatience for liberty" (50).

Gestures of solidarity bring people together at the point where the inevitability of shortcomings and failures meets and determines to co-exist with commitment to critically, creatively, and continually *come back together* in the face of the limitations, constraints, and lack from which that inevitability springs. What broader feminist political potential might be contained in that commitment?

Notes

1 As Elena Cuffari puts it, "[G]estural behavior finds its intelligibility by conforming to certain collectively held standards on multiple levels" (Cuffari 2012, 600).
2 Merleau-Ponty uses the example of his own house in elucidating this point:

> When I move about my house, I know without thinking about it that walking towards the bathroom means passing near the bedroom, that looking at the window means having the fireplace on my left, and in this small world each gesture, each perception is immediately located in relation to a great number of possible co-ordinates.
>
> (1966, 129–130)

3 Later in the same chapter, Merleau-Ponty reiterates this point: "[I]n order to express it, the body in the last analysis must become the thought or intention that it signifies for us" (1966, 197).

4 When I refer to "transmitting meaning," here I am invoking, as I did in the book's Introduction, Lina Insana's analysis of Primo Levi's efforts to meaningfully convey his experience of Auschwitz (see Insana 2009).

5 Like all human relationships, friendship is a relation of power and therefore not immune from normalization; this book recounts multiple instances in which victims/survivors of sexual violence were turned on or treated with indifference after they told friends or friends otherwise learned of their experiences.

6 As I note in Chapter 3, I mark a distinction between the #MeToo phenomenon and Burke's use of "Me Too." Burke has recently voiced concern about the scope, direction, and, therefore, the future, of #MeToo. "Everybody," she relates, is "trying to couch everything under #MeToo." While she recognizes the interconnection of sexual violence with other oppressive practices, Burke nonetheless wants to resist and, indeed, reverse what she sees as the dilution of Girls for Gender Equity's focus: alleviating the effects of and ultimately eradicating sexual violence, especially among women of color and socioeconomically disenfranchised women (see Garber 2018).

7 Burke also sees this focus on (especially famous) individuals and their (sensationalized) stories threatening to undermine the objectives of her work. She recounts that as she watched the hashtag go viral she was already worrying about it "overshadowing" the efforts of grassroots activists (Ohlheiser 2017). It is noteworthy, in light of what I present in Chapter 3 concerning its largely white and privileged character that #MeToo originated in not merely the overshadowing but the actual appropriation of the long-term work of a Black woman.

8 Inter-relational gestures of solidarity can be identified within the protests I analyze in Chapters 3 and 4 as well.

9 See Wilde (2019). I am grateful to my colleague, Deniz Durmus, for encouraging me to analyze Gallagher's and Archila's confrontation of Flake.

References

Ahmed, Sara. 2016. "Interview with Judith Butler." *Sexualities* 19 (4): 482–492.
———. 2017. *Living a Feminist Life*. Durham, NC: Duke University Press.
Arendt, Hannah. 1973. *The Origins of Totalitarianism*. New York: Harvest Books.
Bartky, Sandra. 1990. *Femininity and Domination*. New York: Routledge.
———. 2002. *Sympathy and Solidarity and Other Essays*. New York: Rowman and Littlefield.
Bennet, Jessica. 2017. 'When Saying "Yes" Is Easier Than Saying "No."' nytimes.com, December 16, 2017. www.nytimes.com/2017/12/16/sunday-review/when-saying-yes-is-easier-than-saying-no.html
Bennet, Jessica and Daniel Jones. 2018. "45 Stories of Sex and Consent on Campus." nytimes.com, May 10, 2018. www.nytimes.com/interactive/2018/05/10/style/sexual-consent-college-campus.html
Bergoffen, Debra. 2013. *Contesting the Politics of Genocidal Rape: Affirming the Dignity of the Vulnerable Body*. New York: Routledge.
———. 2017. "Why Rape? Lessons from *The Second Sex*." In *A Companion to Simone de Beauvoir*, edited by Laura Hengehold and Nancy Bauer, 311–324. Hoboken, NJ: Wiley-Blackwell.
Brison, Susan. 2011. "An Open Letter from Black Women to SlutWalk Organizers." huffpost.com, www.huffingtonpost.com/susan-brison/slutwalk-black-women_b_980215.html
———. 2013. "Justice and Gender-Based Violence." *Revue Internationale de Philosophie* 265 (3): 259–275.
———. 2017. Remarks made in presentation as Scholar in Residence at the National Endowment for the Humanities Summer Institute, "Diverse Philosophical Perspectives on Sexual Violence," Elon University, Elon, North Carolina. June 2017.
Brockes, Emma. 2018. '#MeToo Founder Tarana Burke: "You Have to Use Your Privilege to Serve Other People."' theguardian.com, January 15, 2015. www.theguardian.com/world/2018/jan/15/me-too-founder-tarana-burke-women-sexual-assault
Burke, Tarana. 2018. "Me Too is a Movement, Not a Moment." TED.com, www.ted.com/talks/tarana_burke_me_too_is_a_movement_not_a_moment?language=en
Butler, Judith. 1990. *Gender Trouble: Feminism and the Subversion of Identity*. New York: Routledge.
———. 1993. *Bodies That Matter*. New York: Routledge.
———. 2004. "Bodies and Power Revisited." In *Feminism and the Final Foucault*, edited by Dianna Taylor and Karen Vintges, 183–194. Urbana, IL: University of Illinois Press.

———. 2005. *Giving an Account of Oneself.* New York: Fordham University Press.

———. 2010. *Frames of War: When is Life Grievable?* London: Verso.

———. 2015. *Notes Toward a Performative Theory of Assembly.* Cambridge, MA: Harvard University Press.

Cahill, Ann J. 2001. *Rethinking Rape.* Ithaca, NY: Cornell University Press.

Carette, Jeremy. 1999. *Religion and Culture: Michel Foucault.* New York: Routledge.

Celis, William. 1990. "Date Rape and a List at Brown." nytimes.com, November 18, 1990. www.nytimes.com/1990/11/18/us/date-rape-and-a-list-at-brown.html

Chira, Susan and Catrin Einhorn. 2017. "How Tough Is It to Change a Culture of Harassment? Ask Women at Ford." nytimes.com, December 19, 2017. www.nytimes.com/interactive/2017/12/19/us/ford-chicago-sexual-harassment.html

Contreras, Russell. 2011. "Inspired by Toronto Officer's Remark, SlutWalks Spread to U.S. Streets." theglobeandmail.com, May 6, 2011. https://web.archive.org/web/20110509182204/http://www.theglobeandmail.com/news/world/americas/inspired-by-toronto-officers-remark-slutwalks-spread-to-us-streets/article2012312/

Cuffari, Elena Claire. 2012. "Gestural Sense-making: Hand Gestures as Intersubjective Linguistic Enactments." *Phenomenology and the Cognitive Sciences* 11: 599–622.

———. 2016. "Meaning Well: The Interactive Art of Gesturing." *Chiasmi International* 18: 233–246.

Da Silva, Michelle. 2017. "Emma Sulkowicz Isn't Done Making Art About Rape." nowtoronto.com, March 13, 2017. https://nowtoronto.com/art-and-books/art/mattress-performance-artist-emma-sulkowicz-not-done-making-art-about-rape/

Davis, Angela. 1998. "Violence Against Women and the Ongoing Challenge to Racism." In *The Angela Y. Davis Reader,* edited by Joy James, 138–148. Malden, MA: Blackwell Publishers.

Dawson, Graham. 2008. *Making Peace with the Past? Memory, Trauma, and the Irish Troubles.* Manchester: Manchester University Press.

Dines, Gail and Wendy J. Murphy, "SlutWalk is Not Sexual Liberation." theguardian.com, May 8, 2011. www.theguardian.com/commentisfree/2011/may/08/slutwalk-not-sexual-liberation

Donegan, Moira. 2018. "I Started the Media Men List. My Name is Moira Donegan." thecut.com, January 10, 2018. www.thecut.com/2018/01/moira-donegan-i-started-the-media-men-list.html

Du Toit, Louise. 2009. *A Philosophical Investigation of Rape: The Making and Unmaking of the Feminine Self.* New York: Routledge.

Edwards, Stassa. 2014. "Carry that Weight: The Revival of Feminist Performance Art." thehairpin.com, September 29, 2014. www.thehairpin.com/2014/09/carry-that-weight-the-revival-of-feminist-performance-art/

Fenwick, Ben and Alan Schwarz. 2015. "In Rape Case of Oklahoma Officer, Victims Hope Conviction Will Aid Cause." nytimes.com, December 12, 2015. www.nytimes.com/2015/12/12/us/daniel-holtzclaw-oklahoma-police-rape-case.html

Fernandez, Manny. 2019. "'You Have to Pay with Your Body': The Hidden Nightmare of Sexual Violence on the Border.' nytimes.com, March 3, 2019. www.nytimes.com/2019/03/03/us/border-rapes-migrant-women.html

Ford, Matt. 2015. "A Guilty Verdict for Daniel Holzclaw." theatlantic.com, December 11, 2015. www.theatlantic.com/politics/archive/2015/12/daniel-holtzclaw-trial-guilty/420009/

Foucault, Michel. 1980a. "Power, Moral Values, and the Intellectual." Interview with Michael Bess (November 3, 1980), IMEC (Institut Mémoirs de l'Edition Contemporaine) Archive folder number FCL2.A02-06.

———. 1980b. "Christianity and Confession." IMEC (Institut Mémoirs de l'Edition Contemporaine) Archive folder number FCL 3.4/FCL2. A03-04.

———. 1980c. "What is Enlightenment?" In *The Foucault Reader*, edited by Paul Rabinow, 32–50. New York: Pantheon.

———. 1983a. "The Subject and Power." In *Michel Foucault: Beyond Structuralism and Hermeneutics*, 2nd ed., edited by Hubert L. Dreyfus and Paul Rabinow, 208–226. Chicago: University of Chicago Press.

———. 1983b. "On the Genealogy of Ethics: An Overview of Work in Progress." In *Michel Foucault: Beyond Structuralism and Hermeneutics*, 2nd ed., edited by Hubert L. Dreyfus and Paul Rabinow, 229–252. Chicago: University of Chicago Press.

———. 1985. "Final Interview." *Raritan: A Quarterly Review* 5 (1): 1–13.

———. 1990a. *The History of Sexuality, Volume One*. Translated by Robert Hurley. New York: Vintage.

———. 1990b. *The Use of Pleasure: The History of Sexuality, Volume Two*. Translated by Robert Hurley. New York: Vintage.

———. 1994. *The Order of Things*. Translated by Alan Sheridan. New York: Vintage.

———. 1996. "How Much Does It Cost for Reason to Tell the Truth?" In *Foucault Live*, edited by Sylvère Lotringer, 348–362. New York: Semiotext(e).

———. 1997a. "What is Critique?" In *The Politics of Truth*, edited by Sylvère Lotringer and Lysa Hochroth, 23–82. New York: Semiotext(e).

———. 1997b. "What is Revolution?" In *The Politics of Truth*, edited by Sylvère Lotringer and Lysa Hochroth, 83–100. New York: Semiotext(e).

———. 2005. *The Hermeneutics of the Subject, Lectures at the Collège de France, 1981–1982*, edited by Frédéric Gros, translated by Graham Burchell. New York: Palgrave.

———. 2010. *The Government of Self and Others, Lectures at the Collège de France, 1982–1983*, edited by Frédéric Gros, translated by Graham Burchell. New York: Palgrave.

———. 2011. *The Courage of Truth, Lectures at the Collège de France, 1983–1984*, edited by Frédéric Gros, translated by Graham Burchell. New York: Palgrave.

———. 2014. *On the Government of the Living, Lectures at the Collège de France, 1979–1980*, edited by Michel Snellart, translated by Graham Burchell. New York: Palgrave.

Garber, Megan. 2018. "Is #MeToo Too Big?" theatlantic.com, July 4, 2018. www.theatlantic.com/entertainment/archive/2018/07/is-metoo-too-big/564275/

Gavey, Nicola. 2005. *Just Sex? The Cultural Scaffolding of Rape*. New York: Routledge.

Gillis, Wendy. 2013. "A Family's Tragedy and a Town's Shame." thestar.com, April 12, 2013. www.thestar.com/news/canada/2013/04/12/rehtaeh_parsons_a_familys_tragedy_and_a_towns_shame.html

Gilson, Erinn C. 2014. *The Ethics of Vulnerability*. New York: Routledge.

Gore, Sydney. 2018. "Amber Rose on How the SlutWalk Became Part of Her Life's Work." highsnobiety.com, October 5, 2018. www.highsnobiety.com/p/amber-rose-slut-walk-interview/

Graham, Kathryn, Sharon Bernards, D. Wayne Osgood, Antonia Abbey, Michael Parks, Andrea Flynn, Tara Dumas, and Samantha Wells. 2014. '"Blurred Lines?" Sexual Aggression and Barroom Culture.' *Alcoholism: Clinical and Experimental Research* 38 (5): 1416–1424.

Guenther, Lisa. 2012. "Resisting Agamben: The Biopolitics of Shame and Humiliation." *Philosophy and Social Criticism* 38 (1): 59–79.

Habermas, Jurgen. 1999. *Moral Consciousness and Communicative Action*. Cambridge, MA: MIT Press.

Harris, Aisha. 2018. "She Founded Me Too. Now She Wants to Move Past the Trauma." nytimes.com, October 15, 2018. www.nytimes.com/2018/10/15/arts/tarana-burke-metoo-anniversary.html

Harris, Elizabeth A. 2019. "R. Kelly Charged with Ten Counts of Sexual Abuse in Chicago." nytimes.com, February 22, 2019. www.nytimes.com/2019/02/22/arts/music/r-kelly-charged-indicted.html

Hartsock, Nancy. 1990. "Foucault on Power: A Theory for Women?" In *Feminism/Postmodernism*, edited by Linda J. Nicholson, 157–175. New York: Routledge.

Hatab, Lawrence. 2005. *Nietzsche's Life Sentence: Coming to Terms with Eternal Recurrence*. New York: Routledge.

Hay, Carol. 2017. "Enabling the Sociopathy No More." dailynous.com, November 21, 2017. http://dailynous.com/2017/11/21/philosophers-art-morally-troubling-artists/#Hay

Hekman, Susan J. 1996. "Introduction." In *Feminist Interpretations of Michel Foucault*, edited by Susan J. Hekman, University Park, PA: Penn State Press.

Hernandez, Salvador. 2016. 'Daniel Holtzclaw Breaks Silence, Says He "Never Sexually Assaulted Anyone."' buzzfeednews.com, May 20, 2016. www.buzzfeednews.com/article/salvadorhernandez/daniel-holtzclaw-breaks-silence-says-he-never-sexually-assau

Heyes, Cressida J. 2016. "Dead to the World: Rape, Unconsciousness, and Social Media." *Signs* 41 (2): 361–383.

Hill, Zahara. 2017. 'A Black Woman Created the "Me Too" Campaign Against Sexual Assault Ten Years Ago.' ebony.com, October 8, 2017. www.ebony.com/news/black-woman-me-too-movement-tarana-burke-alyssa-milano/

Insana, Lina N. 2009. *Arduous Tasks: Primo Levi, Translation, and the Transmission of Holocaust Testimony*. Toronto: University of Toronto Press.

Joseph, George and Jon Swaine. 2014. 'Behind Columbia's "Rape Lists": When Existing Systems Fail, What Then?' theguardian.com, June 26, 2014. www.theguardian.com/education/2014/jun/26/columbia-university-students-rape-list-mishandle-sexual-assault

Jucliu. 2008a. "The Date Rape List, Part 1." YouTube video, July 14, 2008, 7:16. www.youtube.com/watch?v=O09qTsMX2hc

Jucliu. 2008b. "The Date Rape List, Part 2." YouTube video, July 14, 2008, 3:50. www.youtube.com/watch?v=QnuXokKdJlo&t=40s

Kantor, Jodi and Megan Twohey. 2017. "Harvey Weinstein Paid Off Sexual Harassment Accusers for Decades." nytimes.com, October 5th, 2017. www.nytimes.com/2017/10/05/us/harvey-weinstein-harassment-allegations.html?module=inline

Kantor, Jodi. 2018. "How Saying #MeToo Changed Their Lives." nytimes.com, June 28, 2018. www.nytimes.com/interactive/2018/06/28/arts/metoo-movement-stories.html

Karasek, Sofie. 2018. "I'm a Campus Sexual Assault Activist. It's Time to Reimagine How We Punish Sex Crimes." nytimes.com, February 22, 2018. www.nytimes.com/2018/02/22/opinion/campus-sexual-assault-punitive-justive.html

Kingkade, Tyler. 2014. "Brown University Faces Federal Complaint for Allowing Rapist Back on Campus." huffpost.com, May 22, 2104. www.newyorker.com/magazine/2018/02/12/is-there-a-smarter-way-to-think-about-sexual-assault-on-campus

Lakshmi, Padma. 2018. "I Was Raped at 16 and I Kept Silent." nytimes.com, September 25, 2018. www.nytimes.com/2018/09/25/opinion/padma-lakshmi-sexual-assault-rape.html

Lindsey, Karen, Holly Newman, and Fran Taylor. 2000. "Rape: The All American Crime." In *Dear Sisters: Dispatches from the Women's Liberation Movement*, edited by Rosalyn Baxandall and Linda Gordon, 195–196. New York: Basic Books.

Lindsey, Treva. 2015. "The Rape Trial Everyone in America Should Be Watching." cosmopolitan.com, November 10, 2015. www.cosmopolitan.com/politics/a49050/daniel-holtzclaw-trial-oklahoma/

Littleton, Heather, Amie Grills, and Danny Axsom. 2009. "Impaired and Incapacitated Rape Victims: Assault Characteristics and Post-Assault Experiences." *Violence and Victims* 24 (4): 439–457.

Liu, Julia C. and Alison Klayman. 2014. "Brown's 'Rape List,' Revisited." nytimes.com, September 24, 2014. www.nytimes.com/2014/09/25/opinion/browns-rape-list-revisited.html

Lussenhop, Jessica. 2015. 'Daniel Holtzclaw Trial: Standing with "Imperfect" Accusers.' bbc.com, November 13, 2015. www.bbc.com/news/magazine-34791191

MacKinnon, Catharine A. 2018. "#MeToo Has Done What the Law Could Not." nytimes.com, February 4, 2018. www.nytimes.com/2018/02/04/opinion/metoo-law-legal-system.html

Macur, Juliet and Nate Schweber. 2012. "Rape Case Unfolds on Web and Splits City." nytimes.com, December 16, 2012. www.nytimes.com/2012/12/17/sports/high-school-football-rape-case-unfolds-online-and-divides-steubenville-ohio.html

Malveaux, Suzanne and Veronica Stracqualursi. 2018. "Flake Confronted by Two Female Protesters after Announcing He'll Back Kavanaugh." cnn.com, September 28, 2018. www.cnn.com/2018/09/28/politics/jeff-flake-protesters-kavanaugh-vote/index.html

Marcus, Sharon. 1992. "Fighting Bodies, Fighting Words: A Theory and Politics of Rape Prevention." In *Feminists Theorize the Political*, edited by Judith Butler and Joan W. Scott, 385–403. New York: Routledge.

Margalit, Avishai. 1998. *The Decent Society*. Translated by Naomi Goldblum. Cambridge, MA: Harvard University Press.

McDonough, Katie. 2014. "Brown University Lets Rapist Who Choked His Victim Reenroll After a Semester-long Suspension." salon.com, April 24, 2014. www.salon.com/2014/04/24/brown_university_lets_rapist_who_choked_his_victim_reenroll_after_a_semester_long_suspension/

McKinley, Jr., James C. 2018. "Harvey Weinstein Indicted on Rape and Criminal Sex Act Charges." nytimes.com, May 30, 2018. www.nytimes.com/2018/05/30/nyregion/weinstein-indicted-rape.html

McLaughlin, Eliot C., Sara Sidner, and Michael Martinez. 2016. "Oklahoma City Cop Convicted of Rape Sentenced to 263 Years in Prison." cnn.com, January 22, 2016. www.cnn.com/2016/01/21/us/oklahoma-city-officer-daniel-holtzclaw-rape-sentencing/index.html

Mead, Rebecca. 2015 "Two Beds and the Burdens of Feminism." newyorker.com, April 6, 2015. www.newyorker.com/culture/cultural-comment/two-beds-and-the-burdens-of-feminism

Merleau-Ponty, Maurice. 1963. *Praise of Philosophy and Other Essays.* Translated by John Wild and James Edie. Evanston, IL: Northwestern University Press.

———. 1966. *Phenomenology of Perception.* Translated by Colin Smith. London: Routledge and Kegan Paul.

———. 1973. *The Prose of the World,* edited by Claude Lefort, translated by John O'Neill. Evanston, IL: Northwestern University Press.

Millar, Sarah. 2011. 'Police Officer's Remarks at York Inspire "SlutWalk."' thestar.com, March 17, 2011. www.thestar.com/news/gta/2011/03/17/police_officers_remarks_at_york_inspire_slutwalk.html

Mills, Charles W. 1997. *The Racial Contract.* Ithaca, N.Y.: Cornell University Press.

Mitra, Namrata. 2018. "Routine Unrecognized Sexual Violence in India." In *New Feminist Perspectives on Embodiment,* edited by Clara Fisher and Luna Dolezal, 183–200. New York: Palgrave.

Nietzsche, Friedrich. 1974. *The Gay Science.* Translated by Walter Kaufmann. New York: Vintage.

———. 1979. "On Truth and Lies in a Nonmoral Sense." In *Philosophy and Truth: Selections from Nietzsche's Notebooks of the Early 1870s,* edited and translated by Daniel Breazeale, 79–97. Amherst, N.Y.: Humanity Books.

———. 1989a. *On the Genealogy of Morals.* Translated by Walter Kaufmann. New York: Vintage.

———. 1989b. *Beyond Good and Evil.* Translated by Walter Kaufmann. New York: Vintage.

———. 2003. *Twilight of the Idols.* Translated by R. J. Hollingdale. New York: Penguin.

Nilsen, Ella. 2018. '"This Brings Back So Much Pain": Why So Many Women Saw Themselves in Christine Blasey Ford's Story of Sexual Assault.' vox.com, September 27, 2018. www.vox.com/2018/9/27/17910044/christine-blasey-ford-brett-kavanaugh-sexual-assault-allegations-senate-testimony

North, Anna. 2018. "The Aziz Ansari Story is Ordinary. That's Why We Have to Talk About It." vox.com, January 16, 2018. www.vox.com/identities/2018/1/16/16894722/aziz-ansari-grace-babe-me-too

Ohlheiser, Abby. 2017. 'The Woman Behind "Me Too" Knew the Power of the Phrase When She Created It – 10 Years Ago.' washingtonpost.com, October 19, 2017. www.washingtonpost.com/news/the-intersect/wp/2017/10/19/the-woman-behind-me-too-knew-the-power-of-the-phrase-when-she-created-it-10-years-ago/?utm_term=.f595f714f754

Planty, Michael, Lynn Langton, Christopher Krebs, Marcus Berzofsky, and Hope Smiley-McDonald. 2016. "Female Victims of Sexual Violence." bjs.gov, May 31, 2016. https://www.bjs.gov/content/pub/pdf/fvsv9410.pdf

Raman, Sheela. 2004. "Rape List, Serving the Brown Community Since 1991." browndailyherald.com, September 22, 2004. www.browndailyherald.com/2004/09/22/rape-list-serving-the-brown-community-since-1991/

Redden, Molly and Lauren Gambino. 2015. "Oklahoma Officer's Trial Defense Attacks Credibility of Vulnerable Black Women." theguardian.com, November 27, 2015. www.theguardian.com/us-news/2015/nov/27/oklahoma-officer-daniel-holtzclaw-trial-defense-attacks-credibility-of-vulnerable-black-women

Rol G. 2013. 'Steubenville High School Lout Ridicules "Dead" Rape Victim.' YouTube video, January 4, 2013. www.youtube.com/watch?v=u1Mymae6oDQ&bpctr=1552337843

Scarry, Elaine. 1985. *The Body in Pain: The Making and Unmaking of the World.* New York: Oxford University Press.

Schmitz, Melanie. 2015. "Daniel Holtzclaw Used Race to Bully His Victims Into Submission & His Victims Know Exactly Why." bustle.com, December 11, 2015. https://www.bustle.com/articles/129452-daniel-holtzclaw-used-race-to-bully-his-victims-into-submission-his-victims-know-exactly-why

Simpson, Connor. 2013. "The Steubenville Victim Tells Her Story." theatlantic.com, March 16, 2013. www.theatlantic.com/national/archive/2013/03/steubenville-victim-testimony/317302/

Smith, Roberta. 2014. "In a Mattress, A Lever for Art and Political Protest." nytimes.com, September 22, 2014. www.nytimes.com/2014/09/22/arts/design/in-a-mattress-a-fulcrum-of-art-and-political-protest.html

Snellart, Michel. 2014. "Course Context." In *On the Government of the Living, Lectures at the Collège de France, 1979–1980*, edited by Michel Snellart, translated by Graham Burchell, 326–347. New York: Palgrave.

Sollee, Kristen. 2017. "Five Sex-Positive Takeaways from Amber Rose's SlutWalk." bustle.com, October 30, 2017. www.bustle.com/p/5-sex-positive-takeaways-from-amber-roses-slutwalk-2758195

Stampler, Laura. 2011. "SlutWalks Sweep the Nation." huffpost.com, April 20, 2011. www.huffingtonpost.com/2011/04/20/slutwalk-united-states-city_n_851725.html

"Steubenville: Revelry Turned into Rape." abcnews.com. https://abcnews.go.com/2020/video/steubenville-revelry-turned-rape-18795386

Taylor, Dianna. 2009. "Resisting the Subject: A Feminist-Foucauldian Approach to Countering Sexual Violence." *Foucault Studies* 16: 88–103.

———. 2013. 'Toward a Feminist "Politics of Ourselves."' In *A Companion to Foucault*, edited by Christopher Falzon, Timothy O'Leary, and Jana Sawicki, 403–418. Hoboken, NJ: Wiley-Blackwell.

———. 2018a. "Are Women's Lives (Fully) Grievable? Gendered Framing and Sexual Violence." In *New Feminist Perspectives on Embodiment*, edited by Clara Fischer and Luna Dolezal, 147–165. New York: Palgrave.

———. 2018b. "Humiliation as a Harm of Sexual Violence: Feminist Versus Neoliberal Perspectives." *Hypatia* 33 (3): 434–450.

Taylor, Kate. 2015. "Mattress Protest at Columbia University Continues Into Graduation Event." nytimes.com, May 19, 2015. www.nytimes.com/2015/05/20/nyregion/mattress-protest-at-columbia-university-continues-into-graduation-event.html

Testa, Jessica. "The 13 Women Who Accused a Cop of Sexual Assault, In Their Own Words." buzzfeednews.com, December 10, 2015. www.buzzfeednews.com/article/jtes/daniel-holtzclaw-women-in-their-ow

Tillet, Salamishah. 2011. "What to Wear to a SlutWalk." thenation.com, September 28, 2011. www.thenation.com/article/what-wear-slutwalk/

Tolentino, Jia. 2018. "Is there a Smarter Way to Think about Sexual Assault on Campus?" newyorker.com, February 12, 2018. www.newyorker.com/magazine/2018/02/12/is-there-a-smarter-way-to-think-about-sexual-assault-on-campus

Traister, Rebecca. 2011. "Ladies, We Have a Problem." nytimes.com, July 24, 2011. www.nytimes.com/2011/07/24/magazine/clumsy-young-feminists.html

U.S. Congress. 2018. "Senate Judiciary Committee, Hearing on the Nomination of Brett M. Kavanaugh to be an Associate Justice of the Supreme Court, Day 5, Focusing on Allegations of Sexual Assault." 115th Congress, September 27, 2018. www.washingtonpost.com/news/national/wp/2018/09/27/kavanaugh-hearing-transcript/?utm_term=.566c292e03b7

Van Allen, Lisa. 2019. "I Survived R. Kelly Again and Again." nytimes.com, February 25, 2019. www.nytimes.com/2019/02/25/opinion/r-kelly-survivor-lisa-vanallen.html

Vesoulis, Abby. 2018. "Meet One of the Women Who Helped Change Jeff Flake's Mind in a Senate Elevator." time.com, October 2, 2018. http://time.com/5412444/jeff-flake-elevator-protester/

Walters, Suzanna Danuta. 2018a. "Why Can't We Hate Men?" washingtonpost.com, June 8, 2018. www.washingtonpost.com/opinions/why-cant-we-hate-men/2018/06/08/f1a3a8e0-6451-11e8-a69c-b944de66d9e7_story.html?utm_term=.0693b1094993

———. 2018b. "Mob Misogyny is Nothing New: I Have the Death Threats to Prove It." washingtonpost.com, September 20, 2018. www.washingtonpost.com/opinions/mob-misogyny-is-nothing-new-i-have-the-death-threats-to-prove-it/2018/09/20/7193574a-b21c-11e8-aed9-001309990777_story.html?utm_term=.921b95898d1f

Way, Katie. 2018. "I Went on a Date with Aziz Ansari. It Turned into the Worst Night of My Life." babe.net, January 13, 2018. https://babe.net/2018/01/13/aziz-ansari-28355

West, Carolyn M. and Kalimah Johnson. 2016. "Sexual Violence in the Lives of African American Women." vawnet.org. https://vawnet.org/sites/default/files/materials/files/2016-09/AR_SVAAWomenRevised.pdf

Wilde, Olivia. 2019. *Dare I Say*, Episode Four: "Courage is Contagious." harpersbazaar.com, March 15, 2019. www.harpersbazaar.com/culture/features/a26471077/dare-i-say-podcast/?utm_campaign=socialflowFBHBZ&utm_medium=social-media&utm_source=facebook&fbclid=IwAR0T5uomzDrNRPpojtMpNSjRNC-_SJJBiCDGlGAJ5kOwiBP4nS4luxNqP-4

Williamson, Elizabeth, Rebecca R. Ruiz, Emily Steele, Grace Ashford, and Steve Eder. 2018. "For Christine Blasey Ford, A Drastic Turn from a Quiet Life in Academia." nytimes.com September 19, 2018. www.nytimes.com/2018/09/19/us/politics/christine-blasey-ford-brett-kavanaugh-allegations.html

Yang, Linda. 2017. "'Mattress Girl' Emma Sulkowicz Is Back – and Channeling Her Rage Through BDSM.' broadly.vice.com, May 25, 2017. https://broadly.vice.com/en_us/article/d3gqaw/mattress-girl-emma-sulkowicz-is-backand-channeling-her-rage-through-bdsm

Young, Iris Marion. 1990. *Justice and the Politics of Difference*. Princeton, N.J: Princeton University Press.

Zacharek, Stephanie, Eliana Dockterman, and Haley Sweetland Edwards. 2017. "The Silence Breakers." time.com, December 6, 2017. http://time.com/time-person-of-the-year-2017-silence-breakers/

Index